Endorsements

This is an excellent, anointed collection inspired by a spirit of faith in the Giver of life. Each line flows with poignant words of thought. Fresh revelations of God's tenderness come forth through Candice's responses to God's dealings with her. And, just so, each poem will bring a response of laughter, tears, or encouragement within the reader. Joy exudes from the freshness in arrangement of thought. Be blessed in the reading!

—Martha Lange
Bible teacher
Frankston, Texas

As I read Candice's poetry, I began to understand each poem is all about her experiences she's had loving our precious Jesus for many years. Insight into the forever grace God gives us all, opens one's heart to receive—Receive with an opened heart these precious poems and go forward praising God for His Son Jesus! Congratulations, Candice, for being obedient to God's calling and writing this coming best seller book.

—Sherry Mecom
Ordained Minister, American Marriage Ministries
Dallas, Texas

These poems are really good! Candice has a God-given talent to write and I love that she is using it! These poems are truly straight from the Lord. They all have scripture to support each and every one and are very inspirational.

—Brek Lancaster
Fulldose Music Ltd.
Grapevine, Texas

The Holy Spirit has given Candice a unique writing style that will capture your heart with the love of poetry written through God's Word. You will laugh and maybe cry a happy tear or two as you understand God's Word in simple form. Thank you, sis, for being obedient to the call of God.

—Lynda Noble
Last Call Ministries
Aubrey, Texas

RECEIVING ✝ FREEDOM
MINISTRIES

Copyright © 2019, 2021 by Candice Jannise

Published by Receiving Freedom Ministries

Additional copies of this book can be ordered online at:

- amazon.com

- barnesandnoble.com

- receivingfreedom.com

ISBN: 978-0-578-47279-9

Library of Congress Control Number: 2019938900

Jannise, Candice.

God's Love for You & Me, Written in Poetry / Candice Jannise.

First Printing April 2019

Printed in the United States of America

God's Love for You & Me, Written in Poetry

Written by a Walking-Miracle

by Candice Jannise

RECEIVING ✝ FREEDOM
MINISTRIES

Introduction

Please relax, so you can enjoy putting your focus on God and the vastness of His immeasurable love for you in an entertaining, yet compelling way. The poems in this book are reflections of God's love and His instructions for humanity from many different angles.

God knew you before He formed you in your mother's womb. He created you for His pleasure, and He has good things planned for your future. Trust Him and allow your faith to release God to do what He wants to do through you!

As stated on the cover, I am a walking-Miracle. God saved me from a brain aneurysm, a blood transfusion, five brain surgeries, a seizure, and a paralyzing stroke. I am still alive, although the doctors said I would not live before each of the first three surgeries!

God saved me from death so He could use me to inspire you and give you hope through the uplifting messages this book contains.

**The dove under each poem represents God's Holy Spirit.
Do you desire to know more? Do you *truly* want to hear it?**

The referenced scriptures at the bottom of every poem will enhance your study of God's Word and give you a greater insight into the verses than the poem itself can adequately express.

I pray you will receive revelation and knowledge of God and humble yourself as you think about the incalculable cost He paid for you and me through the blood-bought sacrifice of His only begotten Son. The ransom (payment) made by the Lord Jesus is how God provided the way for everyone who believes in His Son, to receive eternal life with Him.

As the sun on the front cover gives light so we can see the beauty of the trees, God's Son brings His light to dispel the darkness in the world so Christians may see the truth and walk in freedom. After we know His truth, it sets us free!

We, us, our, you, and believers, all refer to obedient Christians.

I pray for God's blessings on you!

Candice

Acknowledgments

I thank God for teaching me how to be led by His Spirit, to do what He directs me to do. His direction in my life inspired every poem you will encounter in this book.

Susan Harring, you are a blessing from the Lord in so many ways! Thank you for the beautiful book cover, title page, and your help with the doves. Your friendship and your professional abilities to do your work as unto the Lord—in my opinion—are unparalleled to all others. Your time and your friendship are invaluable!

Mary Bodine, I extend my thanks to you for the enjoyable time walking around the park together as you captured many outstanding author photos and the masterfully painted message on the wall that says:

"God so loved...you."

The powerful message of God's love for each person dramatically changes the lives of those who **choose** to believe it!

Thank you, Derrick Farris, for teaching me how to edit the text through this book, as well as for your comments and suggestions. I love you, son!

Kym Johns at **www.AlaCarteSolutions.net** in Beaumont, Texas, thank you for designing my website that is making this book available to people all over the world!

Many thanks to my sisters, Sherry Mecom, Lynda Noble, Donna Pace, Tammy Rogers, and Robin Sonnier, brother-in-law Carl Noble, niece-in-law Natalie Hill, high school French and English teacher Marilyn Martin, and to my friends who encouraged me in this poetry journey: Sandy Bodeman, Jerry Caspell, Laura Gilley, Brek Lancaster, Tyo Lancaster, Martha Lange, Kenny Maguire, and Jeff Striplin. Thank all of you for your feedback.

I am grateful to my family and friends for your prayers and support that gave me the courage and strength to write these messages from God, as He spoke them to me.

Dedication

I dedicate this book to my big brother Keith Jannise, his wife Sherry, my brother David Jannise, his wife Lisa, my brother Brian Jannise, his wife Charlyn, my children Derrick Farris and Megan Lindsey.

I also dedicate this book to everyone who desires to know more about God the Father, Jesus the Son, and the Holy Spirit—God is all three of these in one!

Foreword

The best way to describe Candice is that she is saturated – immersed and soaked in the Scripture. She is saturated with the Word of God. I have never met anyone who can recall and recite Book, Chapter, and Verse of so many passages of the Bible as precisely, accurately, and easily as she can.

Her commitment of many years of memorizing more Bible verses, along with the references, than anyone I know is remarkable and awe-inspiring. I have told her more than once that she seems like a walking Bible. But this is far beyond a mere intellectual accomplishment; the Word she recites is alive in her like no one I have ever known. She lives and pours out the Living Word of the Lord Jesus Christ with confidence, faith, and joy.

As a teenager, I began to write poetry that reflected my personal views and inner-feelings and have enjoyed the passion of writing throughout my life. When Candice began to share her poetry with me and asked for my assistance in reviewing her work for this book, I was, of course, intrigued and willing. I find her unique rhymes that so beautifully bring the Scriptures to light, even sometimes with a touch of humor, completely enjoyable, thought-provoking, and inspiring.

Through her poetry, Candice shares her faith, hope, and love of the truth of God's Word in a refreshing, entertaining and meaningful way. I have found deeper meaning through her beautiful interpretation of the Scriptures referenced on each page. Her passion and love for God the Father, the Son, and the Holy Spirit is so evident and uplifting. I know you will be amazed and blessed as you read these poems and study the Scripture references. In fact, you, too, will become saturated with the Word of God and will find a new love and appreciation for all He has done for us.

Jerry Caspell
Author of two poetry books & an original music CD
Allen, Texas

It's all about
Jesus!

Contents

✝

Introduction..4

Acknowledgments..5

Dedication...6

Foreword...7

In Remembrance..10

Golden Nuggets From God's Word..............................11

Personal Poems..91

A Few Fun Poems..105

Authoritative Poems..109

Salvation Information......................................115

Also Available!..118

About the Author...119

To the Readers...120

Closing Comments...121

God Loves...You!...122

In Remembrance

In loving memory of my mother, Ruth Madeline MacKay Jannise. Although she departed many years ago, I still feel she deserves to be remembered.

I also want to acknowledge my father, Cleveland Joseph Jannise, Jr. He was still here when I began writing these poems, but he passed away before I finished them.

In remembrance of my dear friend, John Little, who taught me many biblical lessons, just as a Christian dad would.

Golden Nuggets from God's Word

✝

"Abraham, Isaac, and Jacob"

One day we will be sitting in heaven with Abraham, Isaac, and Jacob;
I believe it will be so pleasant there, the ladies won't need to wear makeup.

Our time for ALL eternity with our precious AND righteous Savior
will be so awesome and joyous, we should exhibit our best behavior.

We WILL be ready to enter into the marriage supper of the Lamb,
dressed in the fine linen of righteousness, and honoring the great "I Am."

We will feast at the banquet table where we shall be served;
In heaven, we will receive bountifully MORE than we deserved.

All the Christians who enter are going to worship the Father there;
We will forever live with Him; about the earth, we won't have a care.

With God, every one of our tears will be removed or wiped away,
and with our mouths, we will be praising our Holy God every day.

The elders will say that God should reward His every righteous one;
We are those who receive Jesus, as Lord; we believe He is God's Son.

What a glorious time for the children of God it will be,
to forever abide with our Lord Jesus, the King of Majesty!

**Exodus 3:14-15; Psalms 8:2; Psalms 58:11; Psalms 95:3;
Matthew 8:11; Acts 17:7; Romans 6:23; 1 Thessalonians 4:17;
Revelation 11:18; Revelation 19:8 & Revelation 21:3-4**

"Amazing Grace"

I thank my Lord Jesus for blessing the words I say and write,
as well as for the peaceful sleep He gives to me every night.

It's His supernatural power that will get our house paid off for us;
His amazing grace has a supernatural way of making us victorious.

The faith God has given me I will no longer allow to be held back;
My God WILL lift me above those who come against me, to attack.

Our defeated enemy does not ever triumph over believers like me,
since our faithful Father has already given us such a sweet victory.

— — — — —

God, my soul yearns for You, in this dry AND thirsty land;
You are great, and You want me to obey Your every command.

Thank You for giving me a choice when I genuinely want to be set free;
Freedom comes from my belief in Jesus AND His payment on Calvary!

**Deuteronomy 28:12; Deuteronomy 30:19; Job 22:28;
Psalms 18:48; Psalms 41:11; Psalms 42:2; Psalms 63:1;
Psalms 127:2; Isaiah 55:11; Matthew 9:29; Mark 11:23;
Luke 23:33; John 3:16; John 8:36; 1 Corinthians 15:57;
2 Corinthians 2:14; Ephesians 2:8; Titus 2:11 & 1 John 2:2**

"Anchored Properly"

This paralyzed hand is a lie straight from the pit of hell
because Jesus died on Calvary and HAS made me well.

I declare by the stripes of Jesus, I HAVE been set FREE
and demand those lying symptoms to be removed from me.

Furthermore, I also shout, "Get out of me, cataract,
and do NOT even think about EVER coming back!"

— — — — —

Father, I ask You to keep me anchored properly in You;
Use me for everything in and through me that You want to do.

Thank You, God, for all You will accomplish for Your glory,
by using me to tell others about Your Son's life-saving story!

**Matthew 7:7-8; Matthew 10:1; Mark 11:23;
Luke 2:12-14; John 3:16; 2 Corinthians 5:21
& 1 Peter 2:24**

"Authority in Christ"

When clouds creep into my life and try to block away the Son,
I use my authority in Christ, and I command the problems to run.

I bind the hindrances up and command they go right away;
Then I put my foot down and demanded they will no longer stay.

I loose love, health, AND prosperity from God, with my mouth,
and testify that my living conditions will NOT attempt to go south.

I declare we are going to climb up the spiritual ladder quite high,
and I boldly confess God's promises—that us, He WILL satisfy!

Daily we walk in our Father's truth, with our shield of protection;
No more will we flee from the enemy, for with him, we are done.

Christians have complete victory in Christ Jesus, our awesome Lord;
When we make it to heaven, He will give each of us our REWARD!

**Job 22:28; Proverbs 4:18; Matthew 18:18; Mark 11:23;
Colossians 2:15; Philippians 4:19; James 4:7
& Revelation 22:12**

"Before Y-2-K"

(Before the year 2000)

I have needlessly been down on my luck since long before Y-2-K,
but from now on, God's Word assures me everything will be okay.

The Christian poems I have diligently written by my OWN right hand,
will surely bring me before many GREAT leaders, all across the land.

My righteous, honorable, and faithful Lord has already promised me,
my future will be better than my past, AND He will give me prosperity.

As a matter of fact, by meditating on His inerrant Word night and day,
is yet another valid reason why great success MUST come my way.

Many good things WILL happen because I obey what I am told;
Each time God gives me a command—I act—I am VERY bold.

Some of God's promises will be received AFTER I am with Him, later;
My current troubles are working eternal glory in me that will be greater!

**Deuteronomy 28:8; Joshua 1:8; Psalms 1:1-3;
Proverbs 4:18; Isaiah 1:19; Haggai 2:9;
Romans 8:18 & 2 Corinthians 4:17**

"Believe While You Pray"

Father, I ask for every poem to turn out beautifully,
to show that You are daily doing this work through me.

May all of it be accurately and professionally done,
to demonstrate the power of Your only begotten Son.

Lord, thank You for giving me Your Words to say,
and for using these lyrics to teach others how to pray.

You said if we believe we receive WHILE we petition You,
we will receive our requests that glorify God—and this is true!

**Isaiah 54:11; Jeremiah 1:9; Matthew 7:7-8;
Mark 11:24; John 14:13; 2 Timothy 2:2 & Titus 1:2**

"Birds of a Feather"

Some have said that birds of a feather will always flock together;
It's amazing how God created them to do this in all kinds of weather.

On these thoughts, I was meditating while I was outside just today,
and when I looked up, I saw a group of birds take off and fly away.

Our awesome God stirs up the seas, and He makes the waves roar;
He helps us rise above the storms, as an eagle in the sky does soar.

We should try to be available for one another in every circumstance;
At work, socially, or go to a program where one's child is to dance.

Through horrendous sickness, in great health, prosperity, or poverty,
our eyes must be on our Lord, in faith—so, Jesus, the world can see.

To the righteous, the Lord will not break His unchanging covenant,
for the promises He has given us are genuinely real AND permanent.

We have God's brilliant, unchanging, AND everlasting promise;
Perpetually for every generation, Jesus will ALWAYS be with us.

If you want reassurance, and you desire to be in God's sanctified family,
receiving Jesus as your Lord, is the ONLY way to secure YOUR destiny!

**Job 36:12; Psalms 61:4; Psalms 89:34;
Psalms 91:14; Isaiah 51:15; John 14:6;
Colossians 1:16 & 2 Timothy 2:2**

"Bless Others"

I should NOT worry about our needs, how they will get met;
Jesus is my faithful Lord, and He isn't finished with me yet.

My genuinely generous Provider is my heavenly Father, God;
Therefore, lack was placed under my feet; it's already been shod.

My extravagant and loving Lord is my "More Than Enough";
He has abundantly blessed me, EVEN when things seem rough.

It is God's plan for His people to prosper for all of our days;
His desire is for us to ALWAYS triumph, in His good ways.

Christians are blessed to bless others, praise the Lord; it is so true;
I love to bless people by teaching them how to be "born again," too.

In Jesus' name, I ask for God's perfect will to be done in your life today,
so you will come to know Him exceedingly more, in a profound way!

**Joshua 1:8; 2 Samuel 22:40; Psalms 8:2;
Jeremiah 29:11; Acts 20:35; Romans 10:9;
2 Corinthians 9:8; Ephesians 1:3; Ephesians 3:20;
Philippians 4:19; Colossians 2:15 & 3 John 1:2**

"Body, Listen to Me"

Body, it is now the appointed time for you to listen to me;
By the shed blood of the Lord Jesus, you ARE already free.

Jesus' sinless blood has paid for the price of ALL your sin,
and by receiving Him as my Lord—I will enter HEAVEN.

Until that blessed day, when my loving Savior and I meet,
I will tell this great news to many of the people I will greet.

We need to know the TRUTH, on Cavalry what, FOR us, was done;
We also must confess Jesus as our Lord and believe He is God's Son.

He is the ONLY way to make it into heaven—forever to stay;
If you have not made Jesus your Lord—will you do so today?

The righteous Lord and Savior Jesus will accept you if you do,
and then YOU will also get to live FOREVER with Him, too!

**Luke 23:33; John 1:12; John 6:37; John 8:36;
Romans 10:9; 1 Corinthians 6:20; 1 Peter 2:24
& 1 John 2:2**

"Both Hands I Will Raise"

Most High God, You are so worthy of all my joyful praise;
As I humbly lift my voice to You, BOTH hands I will raise.

Father, You are holy and righteous, clothed in honor and majesty;
You are eternally faithful, triumphant, powerful, and exuding in loyalty.

I have been explicitly made in Jesus' beautiful AND glorious image;
He is successfully leading me on my journey with Him, my pilgrimage.

Lord, I choose to make my dreams MUCH bigger than my enemies,
for I know Your power is available to me because of Your great mercies.

You will always be mightier than any army I will EVER have to face;
You are with me—so those against us must take a losing, second-place.

My dream is to be used to inspire and touch many people's lives for You,
so Your perfect WILL can be finished, when on this earth we are through!

**Psalms 63:4; Psalms 92:4; Psalms 104:1; Psalms 139:14;
Lamentations 3:23, 37-39; 2 Corinthians 2:14 & 2 Peter 1:10**

"Child of My Younger Years"

I speak blessings on you, lovely child of my younger years;
Thinking of your hospital stay makes me fight back a few tears.

I am sorry for the difficulty you are currently going through,
but I also KNOW my faithful God WILL take care of you!

My heartfelt prayer is you'll quickly, and FULLY, recover,
and of God's amazing grace, you WILL soon find or discover.

I bind the Spirit of Infirmity and DEMAND it to leave you right away;
Because of the authority I have been given—sickness CANNOT stay.

Over you, I boldly speak God's blessings of life, health, and peace,
as I—the Holy Spirit's anointing on you, now confidently release.

My precious one, I declare you ARE healed, according to God's Word;
You KNOW this is true because what is written, you have also heard!

**Job 22:28; Matthew 7:7-8; Matthew 18:18;
Mark 11:23; Romans 10:17 & 1 Peter 2:24**

"Children of God"

The Lord is pleased in us who fear Him—in His mercy, we have hope;
He causes us to rise above our problems, not just to BARELY cope.

To those who respectfully fear Him, He gives knowledge of His power,
and from all of our innumerable enemies, He will be our strong tower.

"We are all children of God," someone tried to convince me one day,
but ONLY those born of the PROMISE belong to God, in this way.

To be an adopted child of God, you MUST believe in Jesus' name,
AND confess Him as your Lord—YOUR salvation is why He came.

When Jesus died, the veil that kept us from the Father was torn in two,
so now we can go boldly to His throne of grace, as we are instructed to do.

You can be a child of God by believing His promise or His guarantee;
Confess Jesus as your Lord, believe He rose again, and you will be free!

**Psalms 61:3; Psalms 147:11; Matthew 27:51;
John 1:12; Acts 4:12; Romans 9:8; Romans 10:9-10;
Galatians 3:26 & Galatians 4:5**

"Choose Life"

God will give you your heart's desires when, in Him, you take delight,
by resting in His promises, being like Jesus, and doing what is right.

Blessed is the one who trusts in God and hears the instructions he is told,
for the unique treasure the Master gives to him is worth MORE than gold.

God highly exalts the people, who to Him, will humbly bow down,
but for ALL eternity, the evil-doers WILL be burned underground.

You were offered a choice of life or death; it is YOUR decision to make,
but ONLY the road to LIFE will keep you from making a BIG mistake.

The eternal life our mighty Savior wants us to affectionately embrace
will come from choosing Jesus, and receiving His amazing GRACE!

**Deuteronomy 30:19; Psalms 19:10; Psalms 37:4;
Psalms 40:4; Matthew 3:12; John 1:12; John 3:16
& Romans 5:21**

"Christian Bakers"

Lord God, I now sincerely pray for every godly Christian baker,
who does their beautiful work of art to glorify YOU, their Maker.

The ones who aren't merely doing what they do for money, to attract it,
but they who obey Your Word, and do the work as unto You, every bit.

Their seven-fold return MUST be repaid, and will bless them with more;
It will give them greater honor in the end, than they EVER had before!

The divine blessing of these men and women is undoubtedly from You
because they are obeying Your Word—whatever You told them to do.

In Jesus' mighty name, I bless every genuine Christian baker today,
and thank You for NOT allowing their businesses to be taken away!

**Proverbs 6:31; Isaiah 55:11; Jeremiah 1:12;
Jeremiah 29:11; Luke 11:28 & Colossians 1:16**

"Christians Are Victorious"

In this life Christians currently live in, we do not belong,
and while here, many things against us might go wrong.

Heartbreaks, responsibilities, failures, illnesses, and such,
may hinder us from thinking about the Lord Jesus—much.

There are people using wheelchairs and others, who use canes,
some who cannot see or hear, or have trouble using their brains.

What Christians need to know is we are STILL victorious,
because, in this world, we are just like our Savior, Jesus.

We are MORE than our troubles and our woes;
We are equipped to overcome ALL of these foes.

— — — — —

Since you are more than any debilitating physical circumstance,
trust God for whatever you need; go ahead—take the chance!

Concentrate on the promises God has already given you;
Cast aside all doubt and let your faith PROVE He is true!

God's Word tells us, by Jesus' stripes we WERE healed;
Our genuine faith will allow His Word, in us, to be revealed.

Jesus said to speak to the mountain and believe what you pray,
so if you do these things, in faith, you will have what you say!

Just use your faith in Jesus to ONLY believe;
That's how—from God—you CAN receive!

**Deuteronomy 20:4; Matthew 9:29; Mark 11:23;
Luke 9:1; Ephesians 1:3; Philippians 3:20;
1 Thessalonians 2:13; Hebrews 11:13;
1 Peter 2:24 & 1 John 4:17**

"Complete Restoration"

I speak to my whole body—I confidently talk to my God-given brain;
I command every part of you to be completely restored, in Jesus' name.

Today is the most magnificent day to receive my complete restoration;
God's glory will be manifest on earth; I believe this, without hesitation.

Lift your hands, bend your knees, AND allow yourself to be healed;
Only believe—don't doubt, and Christ's power in you will be revealed.

Jesus paid for you to be well, with the painful stripes He obediently bore;
Thank Jesus for His obedience, and don't suffer from sickness anymore.

I will sing jubilant praises forever to God's holy and righteous name;
Since He has made Himself known to me, I have not been the same.

I look forward to the day when I'll dwell in the Lord's house forever;
I will not want to leave His outstandingly beautiful place—not EVER.

For all eternity in the Lord's house, I will be delighted to live;
My continual thanks to Him I will gratefully ALWAYS give.

Reveal to me Your perfect will, my Father, in Jesus' name I pray;
I ask for wisdom to know what I can do, to stay out of Your way!

**Psalms 23:6; Psalms 61:8; Matthew 7:7-8; Mark 11:23;
2 Corinthians 5:17; 1 Thessalonians 5:18;
Hebrews 12:12-13 & 1 Peter 2:24**

"Created in God's Image"

People are as the Father, Son, and Holy Spirit, is what I am seeing,
as we are also a three-part creation—a body, soul, and spiritual being.

In God's beautiful image is how EVERY person was uniquely made;
Christians get saved from hell because of the price for sin our Jesus paid.

On earth, believers become as Jesus is by letting God's love live inside of us;
If you do not know the message of the cross, perhaps it, we can further discuss.

The Lord Jesus died on the cross to pay for the entire world's unrighteous sin,
but only the people who genuinely confess Him as their Lord ARE born again.

Each Christian's lowly body WILL be transformed into Jesus' glorious one
because we received Him as our Lord AND we believe in what HE has done.

Every person's physical human body will once again return to the dust,
but Christians' Spirits and souls will go to God, since Jesus we did trust.

Those who belong to the Lord Jesus obey the commanding Words He said;
The people who do not obey Him will be punished eternally in hell, instead.

To receive Jesus, turn to the "Prayer of Salvation" on page 117 now;
Say the prayer to accept Jesus as your Lord—I will teach you how.

Oh, what a splendid and triumphant day Jesus' soon return is going to be;
Genuine Christians will begin our new life abiding with God, for ALL eternity!

**Genesis 1:27; Psalms 27:4; John 3:16; 1 Corinthians 6:20;
1 Thessalonians 4:17; 1 Thessalonians 5:23; 2 Thessalonians 1:9;
1 Peter 1:9; 1 John 2:2 & Revelation 21:4**

"Crown of Glory"

Many years ago, I was bald, but my gray hair is now much preferred;
It is a crown of glory—this is what I have learned from God's Word.

Gray hair naturally also comes to people who live a little longer,
and the things we go THROUGH, allow Christ to make us stronger.

In Christians, wisdom is one thing that may come with our silver hair;
Those with this God-given color can one day meet the Lord in the air.

Howbeit, the younger Christians on earth will also meet Him, too;
When the Lord Jesus comes in His glory, will He come for you?

The only way any person—including you—can go with Him
is to be forgiven for your sins—for every single one of them.

Believing Jesus is currently alive will allow God to forgive you today,
if you will sincerely confess Jesus as your Lord, with the words you say.

To the Christians with gray hair—you can show YOUR crown of glory,
as you tell others about God's incarnation—the REAL Christmas story!

**Proverbs 16:31; John 1:1, 14; John 3:16; Romans 10:9-10;
Ephesians 1:7; Philippians 4:13 & 1 Thessalonians 4:16**

"Do Not Be Afraid"

Child of God, do not be afraid nor be dismayed;
The devil lost this battle with the hand he played.

Jesus is triumphant, so to You, Lord, we joyfully sing;
I imagine hearing angels praising God, as the bells ring.

Jesus HAS given us the anointed rain upon our land
and made us victorious, with His righteous right hand.

He gives us strength and has taken out all our foes,
so each enemy is under our feet, including our toes.

Hallelujah, to our Lord and triumphant King Jesus,
who died and victoriously rose again to justify us.

God loved us more than enough to set Christians free,
so through our Lord, He gives us an amazing victory!

**Psalms 8:6; Isaiah 41:10; Luke 2:13;
John 3:16; Romans 4:25; 1 Corinthians 15:57;
Ephesians 2:15; Philippians 4:13 & Colossians 2:15**

"Elijah Heard God's Voice"

Elijah, the great prophet, heard God's voice
and so CAN you—it is also YOUR choice.

In faith, you can ask God to speak to you, and He will,
even if your name is not Joyce, Kenneth, Andrew, or Bill.

You have the perfect opportunity to hear God, and obey;
Your belief in Jesus determines where you WILL always stay.

You decide by believing Jesus is God's Son who rose from the dead,
by confessing Him as your Lord, and believing the words He said.

Choosing Jesus is the ONLY acceptable decision or the ONLY way
that guarantees you will be WITH Him, forever—every single day!

**Deuteronomy 30:19; 1 Samuel 3:9-12; Luke 11:28;
John 3:16; John 14:6; Romans 10:9
& 1 Thessalonians 4:17**

"Everything Works Together for My Good"

Lord, thank You for blessing the work of my hands, and my sight;
Thank You for making everything against me, work out all right.

Thank You, God, for causing everything to be JUST as it should,
and for ultimately making every problem work together for my good.

Lord, I genuinely trust Your plan for me, and I sincerely praise You:
I ask You to do, through me, the tremendous works You desire to do.

You are righteous and powerful, and each believer's soon-coming King,
so we, who are waiting on Your SOON return, can now joyously sing!

**Deuteronomy 28:12; Psalms 47:6; Jeremiah 29:11;
Romans 8:28; 2 Timothy 4:8; James 1:12
& Revelation 22:12**

"Expectant Mothers"

My heart is filled with joy for every Christian couple,
for the husband, whose wife is an expectant mother,
because the little one soon to be born can one day
be to Jesus, a precious sister, or a younger brother.

The unknown treasures and unusual sounds
that each adorable newborn baby brings,
fill the parents' lives with unconditional
love and inexpressible, yet joyful feelings.

There will be many nutritious feedings, peaceful naps,
cozy warm blankets, educational, but fun, pliable toys,
and exciting adventures filled with laughter for these
children, the delicate girls, as well as the chubby boys.

The dependent babies soon become independent
and brave walking children, it's certainly true,
but, mom and dad, the ones to teach your child
about your loving Creator and Savior, are you!

Start training the little one early, to follow Jesus'
inerrant footsteps your little one is to follow,
and when maturity hits, your child will remain
with God, because Christ—he or she WILL know.

If you have received Jesus as your Lord
and Savior, then you are God's child, too,
and even more than you will adore your baby,
does your heavenly Father love and cherish you!

**Deuteronomy 6:6-7; Psalms 85:13; Proverbs 22:6;
Matthew 12:50; Galatians 4:6; Colossians 1:16
& 1 John 4:10**

"Focus on God"

Thank You, my loving Father, for using me for Your purposes today;
When You saved my life for Your glory, it was MORE than okay.

I am shouting loudly with beautiful and melodious praises, for You,
since with Your powerful finger, there's NOTHING that You can't do!

———————

The sinless blood our righteous Lord Jesus obediently shed for us,
has washed away every Christian's sins and made us victorious!

When we confess Jesus, we get a new life, and God purges away our sin;
He grants all who receive His Son, Jesus, the right into heaven—to enter in!

Jesus will lead us to fountains of living waters, which will satisfy our thirst,
because—while we lived in our human body—we put our GOD FIRST!

The glory God WILL reveal in us will make the problems quickly dim;
They won't disturb us anymore because we now choose to focus on HIM!

**Exodus 8:19; Matthew 10:32; Romans 8:18; Romans 9:17;
Romans 10:9; 2 Corinthians 5:17-21; Galatians 3:26;
Ephesians 1:7; Philippians 2:8; Hebrews 1:3; Revelation 1:5
& Revelation 7:17**

"Friend in the Lord"

In Jesus' name, I bless my friend in the Lord,
and I pray she will receive her priceless reward.

God, I also ask for her to have a truly blessed day,
and honestly desire for good things to go her way.

Please allow her to continually be drawn closer to You,
and keep her from the evil things the devil wants her to do.

I sincerely bless this misguided person, and I do not curse,
because I don't want her situation to grow ANY worse.

Thank You for Your celestial angels surrounding us all around,
and for the harmonious tunes of triumph, I hear in the background!

**Psalms 34:7; Psalms 91:14; Matthew 7:7-8;
Luke 2:13-14; Romans 12:14; 2 Corinthians 2:14
& Revelation 22:12**

"God Is LOVE"

God wants believers to know how deep, wide, and tall
His extravagant and never-ending love is for us ALL.

God is LOVE; that is who our amazing Creator is today;
He genuinely knows us, in a unique and attentive way.

If you don't know Jesus, invite Him to come into you this day;
Allow Him to wash you clean AND take YOUR sins away.

These words, my heart is screaming, I tell you they are true;
There is a loving Father who desires to make YOU brand-new.

Because God is LOVE, He sent Jesus to die in our rightful place;
Therefore, we who believe in Jesus will SOON see God's face.

Even if your road now seems LONG and is filled with MUCH misery,
Child of God, remember, with Jesus, for ALL eternity, you will be free!

**Psalms 16:11; Psalms 36:5; Psalms 139:13; John 3:16;
John 8:36; Ephesians 3:18-19; 1 Thessalonians 4:17;
1 Peter 1:18-19; 1 Peter 3:18; 2 Peter 3:9; 1 John 4:8;
Revelation 21:3-4 & Revelation 22:4**

"God Lifts Me Much Higher"

The Lord, my God, lifts me much higher than my enemy;
He fights all of my battles, and He gives me each victory.

It is morning, and soothing comfort has now gently embraced me;
The weeping I endured is gone, and joyful today is how I will be.

I exchanged my painful sorrow for the anointed Son's pure joy;
All my jubilant praises to God, I am thankful I can NOW employ.

Lord, You always have a way to make Your people victorious;
To me, that shows You are so amazingly awesome AND glorious.

Thank You for letting me call on You when I have a need or trial;
To make things work out alright, it only takes You a little while!

**Deuteronomy 20:4; Deuteronomy 28:12; Psalms 18:48;
Psalms 27:6; Psalms 30:5; Psalms 50:15;
Isaiah 61:3 & 2 Corinthians 2:14**

"God Makes Us Whole"

I am quite thankful my God causes me in every area of life, to excel,
and for blessing the work of my hands, while equipping me to do well.

When I delight myself in my Lord, He gives me the desires of my heart;
Then, when I fully meditate on Him, He enables me to have a new start.

God speaks peace unto all of His people, His preciously prized saints;
Not to he who grow weary of doing good deeds, and eventually faints.

Our Father, who keeps His children safe from harm, will not ever sleep;
He always works everything out for our good, His faithful little sheep.

Our Deliverer keeps each of us from evil and protects our righteous soul;
He watches us day and night, and He also flawlessly makes us whole!

**Psalms 1:3; Psalms 37:4; Psalms 85:8; Psalms 121:3-8;
Matthew 22:37-39; Romans 8:28; Hebrews 8:10
& James 1:25**

"God Proved His Love"

Thank You, Lord Jesus, for Your love You generously did give,
when You allowed Your body to be sacrificed, so Christians can live.

You indeed are the beloved Son of God, seated at His powerful right hand;
You died so You could make things right, with God and us on this land.

The enmity between God and Christians was broken AND removed;
When You gave up Your life for mankind, Your love, You surely proved.

The Christians You have saved, from hell, will always praise Your name,
for we will ALWAYS be glad You finished the work for which You came!

**Matthew 3:17; Mark 16:19; John 3:16; John 19:30;
2 Corinthians 5:18; Ephesians 2:15;
Hebrews 10:12 & 1 John 2:2**

"God Speaks"

God speaks to me daily; I hear Him when I pray;
The choice is up to me if I will seek Him and obey.

I am free to decide to obey now, or I can wait for another hour,
but the longer I choose to linger, I end up limiting His power.

I must listen intently to Him with my spirit, in my inner man;
This is the way I WILL fully discover my God's perfect plan.

Since my Lord loves me completely, with ALL of His heart,
when I listen to Him, He gives me wisdom, as soon as I start.

"Live the life—or the call, God has for me," His scriptures say;
As I obey Him, my life works better, because I'm living HIS way!

**Deuteronomy 30:19; Job 33:3; Psalms 78:41;
Psalms 85:8; John 3:16; Romans 6:16
& 2 Peter 1:10**

"God Truly Loves You"

God's care for His people goes to an unimaginable and lengthy extent,
He tore the veil that separated us, so He can forgive those who repent.

God meticulously loves you; He knows how many hairs are on your head;
God created you for His pleasure, so He does NOT want you to stay dead.

God's love is undoubtedly beyond what any Christian can understand,
how He sent His Son Jesus, to free us from our sins done on this land.

He has good plans for your future; if you want to know them, ask;
Believe He will answer you, and He WILL show you your task.

Let's put God FIRST, keeping our eyes on Jesus, and we WILL succeed;
Seeking God's kingdom and righteousness first, supplies our EVERY need.

When aggravation suddenly arises from the ominous dark places below,
the triumphant and victorious praises to my Jesus, I will joyfully show.

If you have not yet received Christ Jesus, repent before it is too late;
He is returning SOON, and not much longer will He patiently wait!

**Psalms 150:6; Isaiah 55:9; Jeremiah 1:12;
Jeremiah 29:11; Matthew 6:33; Matthew 7:8, 21-23;
Matthew 10:30; Matthew 14:30; Matthew 27:51;
John 3:16; Romans 9:17; Ephesians 3:20;
1 Thessalonians 2:13; Hebrews 12:2-3; James 1:5;
1 John 2:2 & Revelation 22:20**

"God's Currency"

God, may ALL of Your glorious plans on earth be done,
to the praise, and for the glory, of Your ONLY begotten Son.

I am Your currency, God, so spend me as You will choose;
All of my dreams and desires, I have now decided to lose.

The greatest longing of my heart is for Your kingdom to be revealed,
while believers in You, through my amazing testimony, will be healed.

The unstoppable faith, from You, to believe Your eternal Word,
will come to them by Your truth they now hear—and have heard.

Lively, yet sweet praise, which belongs to my holy and righteous King,
is NOW dramatically rising upward, as I—to You—cheerfully sing!

**Psalms 104:33; Isaiah 40:8; Matthew 6:10;
John 17:17; Acts 17:7; Romans 10:17
& 1 Thessalonians 2:13**

"God's Amazing Grace"

Our deliverance can ONLY be received by God's amazing grace,
for our righteous works cannot EVER take us to His eternal place.

Since God immensely loved the world, including all of its sinners,
He gave His only Son, who died for us, to make Christians winners.

Our redemption was paid for by Jesus' blood, for our unrighteous sin;
What believers must do is confess Jesus as our Lord, to enter heaven!

Our hearts must also believe God raised the Lord Jesus from the dead;
This amazing sacrifice allows those who receive Jesus, to be God-led.

The Lord will always provide abundantly for EACH of His offspring;
After we seek Him, He will supply our needs; we won't lack anything!

**Nehemiah 9:21; Psalms 30:11; Isaiah 55:11; Isaiah 64:6;
Matthew 6:33; Luke 6:23; John 1:12; John 3:16;
Romans 8:14; Romans 10:9; 2 Corinthians 5:17, 21;
Ephesians 1:7; Ephesians 2:8-9; Philippians 4:19;
1 Thessalonians 2:13; Hebrews 4:16 & 1 John 2:2**

"God's Love Cannot Be Measured"

What are the things that are demanding most of your time?
Can you stop for just a little while and listen to my rhyme?

God genuinely loves you; He created you for His good pleasure;
He is always faithful, and His love for you is impossible to measure.

He wants to be man's Provider, Savior, Restorer, and Healer, who is kind;
Have you opened up your HEART to Him yet, and made up your mind?

God is Merciful—His heart yearns for His daughter and also His son,
so go home to the Father (in faith) and quickly, to YOU, He will run!

If you are ready to give Father God your everything, and He is your all,
then sincerely thank Him for picking you up EVERY time that you fall.

He is each Christian's Provider, Savior, Restorer, and Healer, who is kind;
Have you given YOUR heart to Him? Have you made up YOUR mind?

**Proverbs 24:16; Luke 15:20; Ephesians 5:23;
Philippians 4:19; 1 Thessalonians 5:18;
1 Peter 2:24 & Revelation 4:11 (KJV)**

"God's Love Is Perfect"

I should aim to speak gently, and in my decisions, not bend,
because my focus is not merely for the moment, but the end.

I try to rehearse the truth in my thoughts, and say it out loud, too;
Then I notice I am blessed by God, and my day is good when I do.

My right hand teaches me some awesome and amazing things,
by doing my work unto God and waiting for the blessings He brings.

He said He wouldn't keep anything good from me because I walk uprightly;
He showers me with His great love and makes my face shine so brightly.

Do you want this love of God I am currently sharing with you?
Receive Jesus as YOUR Lord today; you'll be pleased if you do.

To you, the Father's mighty arms are now opened, VERY wide;
He is inviting you, while there still is time, to quickly come inside.

God is faithful to His people—so each Christian, He WILL protect,
and He will meet ALL of our needs because His love is PERFECT!

**Psalms 15:4; Psalms 35:27; Psalms 45:4; Proverbs 4:18;
Ecclesiastes 8:1; Matthew 5:48; Philippians 4:19;
2 Thessalonians 3:3 & 1 John 4:17-18**

"God's Magnificent Plans"

God's mighty power is set in motion to work favorably for me today,
according to my confident belief in the right words I CHOOSE to say.

As a result of God's plan, by Jesus' stripes, I've been completely healed;
His irresistible plans to set others free, through me, ARE being revealed.

Did you know, to Himself, ONLY God can draw people from the other cults?
When He does this, they are brought to the Lord with spectacular results!

Every time a believer goes to the Father through the Lord Christ Jesus,
washed clean—by His blood—is how our imaginative Maker sees us.

Jesus is the only way ANYONE can EVER go to our Father God;
This includes Sue, Steve, Billy, Jack, Jim, Willy, Tammy, and Todd!

**Job 22:28; Psalms 45:1; Mark 11:23; John 6:44;
John 14:6; John 15:16; Acts 8:3; Acts 9:18;
Acts 16:25-34; 1 Thessalonians 2:13;
1 Peter 2:24 & Revelation 1:5**

"God's Purpose Will Stand"

When the enemy tries to cause us much pain or unending trouble,
God is quite capable of restoring to us, by His grace—DOUBLE.

The anointed blessing of the loving Father is on you, right now;
Trust in Him, so He can help, and do not worry about "HOW."

God's supply is always larger than any person's heavy demand;
Wholeheartedly trust Him to help you, with His righteous hand.

He will skillfully work things out in a great way, just right for you,
if you use your faith AND work on what He has called you to do.

The Lord's plans and purposes for His chosen ones WILL stand;
To pray, humble ourselves, and seek God, lets Him bless our land.

— — — — —

Lord, I pray our hearts will not attempt to resist You any longer,
and our souls will believe You, and will always become stronger.

In Jesus' mighty name, I ask these requests—and I fervently pray
that both of them will soon be answered, in Your Most Holy Way!

**2 Chronicles 7:14; Isaiah 41:10; Isaiah 61:7;
Jeremiah 29:11; Matthew 7:7; Romans 8:28;
Romans 12:3; 2 Corinthians 3:18;
1 Thessalonians 2:13 & James 5:15**

"God's Righteous Face"

Blessed are those who faithfully keep God's good ways;
He has delightfully blessed them for all of their glorious days.

Lord, inside me, is where I ask for You to take Your rightful place;
One day, I believe I WILL be allowed to see Your righteous face.

I desire to understand COMPLETELY in great detail about You;
To know You intimately, like the way about me, You currently do.

Lord, I genuinely desire to reflect Your brilliantly radiant glow,
so when other people see You in me, the more of You, they will know.

You are loving and infinitely more worthy than ALL the praise
that we can EVER possibly give to You for our length of days.

Your love is MUCH greater than I can comprehend or even imagine,
but when I think about You, my heart QUICKLY begins to gladden.

I am thankful and truly delighted to know You MORE each day;
I will joyfully live in Your presence, where forever, I WILL stay!

**Psalms 21:6; Psalms 61:8; Psalms 145:21;
Proverbs 8:32; Isaiah 55:9; Matthew 10:30;
Ephesians 1:3; 1 Thessalonians 4:17
& Revelation 1:16**

"God's Word Will Feed You"

When there's hurt welling up in your heart, and you need to cry out loud,
your heavenly Father is deeply moved when He sees you in the crowd.

God knows every time you are in overwhelming and unyielding pain;
He wants to remove your ailments—He doesn't want them to remain.

God desires to use His powerful Word to produce good fruit inside of you,
so mix the promises in the Bible ALL together to make a delicious stew.

God's Word that you believe will nourish your body with good health
and will fill your storehouse (your bank account) WITH great wealth.

His proven Word will bring nourishment to all of your three-part being;
Miracles will occur—what you believe of God, is what you'll be seeing.

It is from the good seed you sow expectantly, on moist and fertile ground,
that produces up to a hundredfold return, which for others, can't be found.

The Almighty is lifting you quite high, for HIS irrefutable glory;
He wants you to talk about the life of Jesus and HIS amazing story!

**Joshua 1:8; Psalms 1:2-3; Psalms 3:3; Psalms 18:48;
Proverbs 4:22; Matthew 8:2-4, 13; Matthew 9:29;
Matthew 14:14; Mark 4:20; John 4:32; Acts 3:10;
2 Corinthians 5:18; 1 Thessalonians 5:23
& 2 Timothy 2:2**

"Heaven"

Heaven is not a place for the people who are good, but who are forgiven;
This eternal reward cannot be obtained by good deeds or perfect livin'.

Through faith in Jesus is the ONLY way for us to be in this place forever;
Without receiving Him as Lord before we die, we will see Him, NEVER!

To be made a brand-new creation and forgiven by God today,
confess Jesus as your Lord, with the faith-filled words you say.

Believe the Lord Jesus is the Father's ONLY begotten Son,
and completely trust what the Bible says He has already done.

You will be obedient to Jesus, by obeying the Words God said,
when you have eternal life—so you won't EVER end up dead!

Without Him—to eternal judgment, unbelievers will go,
and the grace of the Almighty God they will NEVER know.

Choosing life, by receiving Jesus and setting yourself free,
will keep you from burning forever in hell, quite miserably.

Jesus will set every born-again believer in HIM, completely free;
He can because He broke the chains that held us—for ALL eternity!

**Isaiah 9:4; Matthew 3:12; John 3:16;
John 8:36; John 11:26; John 14:6, 21-23;
Romans 10:9-10; 2 Corinthians 5:17;
1 Thessalonians 4:17 & Hebrews 5:9**

"He Will Come Through"

God, I know I can certainly always trust You to come through for me
because of Your desire for my good health and provision, I NOW see.

I confidently press into You, and I stretch forth my diligent hand,
as I boldly declare Your eternal love for people, ALL over the land.

Lord, You told Christians to trust You, and we are to ONLY believe;
Each time we don't doubt Your Word—what we ask, we will receive.

Your Words are proven; they will come to pass IF we just hold fast;
They will cause Your blessing on each Christian to permanently last!

God, You will come through for Your children, time AND time again
because Jesus removed our penalty when He paid for ALL our sin!

**2 Samuel 7:29; Psalms 37:5; Proverbs 10:4;
Matthew 7:7-8; Mark 11:24; John 3:16; John 14:6;
Romans 3:24-25; Ephesians 1:3, 7; 1 John 2:2;
3 John 1:2; Revelation 7:17 & Revelation 21:4, 6**

"I Am Free!"

Thank You, Lord Jesus, for the glorious
things You have already done for me.
Thank You, Lord, for my salvation
and for miraculously setting me free.

Thank You that I am free from
sin, death, hell, and also the grave.
Thank You that I am no longer
Satan's worn-out or bound-up slave.

I am free for the entire world to see
Your awesome AND amazing power.
Thank You, Lord, for the great victory
You made possible for THIS very hour.

Thank You, God, for the redeeming blood
of Jesus, which was victoriously shed for me.
Thank You I am healed, saved, and forgiven,
AND by the power of Jesus' blood, I am free!

**Romans 3:24; Romans 6:16;
1 Corinthians 6:20; Colossians 2:15;
Ephesians 1:7; 1 Peter 1:18-19;
1 Peter 2:24 & 1 John 2:2**

"I Boldly Declare"

Father, I ask for You to keep us from evil today,
just as my loving Lord and Savior taught me to pray.

May Your perfectly pre-ordained will be done,
for the glory and the praise of Your obedient Son.

Father, thank You for answering my every prayer,
and for allowing me to have what I boldly declare.

I proclaim that "Daily Blessings from God's Word"
will stir up people's faith from what they have heard.

To the readers of this poetry book, I also pronounce,
"The truths you learn from it—will, the devil, renounce."

The devil is like a lion, who is roaring as he eagerly stops by,
but if a child of God resists him, he WILL FLEE—so, try!

Jesus defeated Satan by telling him what is written in God's Word;
Any attempt to defeat Satan differently than Jesus did, is absurd!

**Job 22:28; Matthew 4:4; Mark 11:23;
John 8:32; John 17:15; Romans 10:17;
Philippians 2:8; James 4:7 & 1 Peter 5:8**

"I Have a Rendezvous"

(A future meeting)—sounds like "Ron-day-voo"

In 2004, I had a brain aneurysm, so the doctor gave my head a shave,
but I am more alive now than before, because my Jesus, me, He did save.

I thank my God for not allowing me to be damaged beyond repair,
for fully restoring my whole body, and for giving me all new hair.

Now that I am a little older, some of the growth is a shiny array of gray;
With this crown of glory from my generous God, I am MORE than okay.

Gray hair, for me, is MUCH better than having no hair at all,
because the numerous dents in my head are NOT very small.

I can walk, talk, and praise God joyfully with a rhyme;
what is your daily routine? How do you invest your time?

Putting the Lord first-place on your daily accustomed to-do list
will allow Him to supply your every need—do you get the gist?

With Christ Jesus in the center of my life, I have been made brand new,
so at the appointed time—with God, in heaven, I have a rendezvous!

**Proverbs 16:31; Matthew 6:33; John 3:16; Acts 17:28;
1 Corinthians 3:7; 2 Corinthians 5:17 & Revelation 21:3**

"I Lift My Hands"

Lord, I will lift my hands in Your most holy name;
Since You touched me, I have NOT been the same.

In innocence, I have thoroughly washed both of my hands;
Now I am ready to share You in ALL of Your great lands.

I bless every part of my body, including my whole brain;
I command every aspect of it to revive—in Jesus' name!

Thank You, Lord, for supernaturally healing and setting me free;
I am thankful for this pre-ordained victory many people will see.

Father God, I lift my hands AND sing melodious praises, too;
I thank You for making me to be a marvelous replica of YOU.

Thank You for teaching me I CAN certainly have whatever I say;
Now I choose to speak words of victory over my loved ones today.

— — — — —

Child of God, do you care to know what I want to say about you and me?
I gladly declare we are righteous, in Christ, AND we are both set free!

Our debt was paid with the sinless blood that was shed by the Lord Jesus;
He paid every Christian's debt, IN FULL, AND completely freed us!

**Genesis 1:27; Psalms 26:6; Psalms 63:4; Mark 11:23;
John 8:36; 2 Corinthians 2:14; Hebrews 10:12;
1 Peter 2:24 & 1 John 4:17**

"Jesus and Heaven"

He is the Son of God, seated at the right hand of the Majesty on High,
but one day, very soon, the Lord will meet His joyous saints in the sky.

Christians will live with Him forever; we will walk on His street of gold;
Everything will be perfect there—we will neither feel too hot nor cold.

The temperatures will be perfect for each Christian, just as they should,
because the moment God created everything, He said that it was all good.

Heaven is full of abounding love, and impressive beauty is all around;
Christians will FOREVER sing praises to God with a melodious sound!

Here, Jesus leads us to the living waters, and our tears are wiped away;
He is our eternal bright light—and with Him, we will ALWAYS stay!

**Genesis 1:31; Psalms 145:2; Matthew 3:17;
1 Thessalonians 4:17; Hebrews 1:3; Revelation 7:17;
Revelation 21:4, 21-23 & Revelation 22:16**

"Jesus' Infinite Atonement"

Jesus paid the price I was not able to pay, AND He made me free;
Because of His infinite atonement, Satan no longer has a hold on me.

I will love my benevolent Lord Christ Jesus for all of my days,
and for eternity, I will GLADLY give Him my jubilant praise!

The payment for sin was made by the LAMB, who was slain;
Now FOREVER, with the Lord Jesus, each Christian will remain.

Jesus' willing obedience to the Father AND His perfect sacrifice
gives every obedient Christian access to heaven—He paid our price!

This is the reason we can shout, "Hallelujah" to the King of kings,
so there is NO wonder as to why each victorious Christian sings!

**Psalms 79:13; Matthew 28:20; John 1:29; John 3:16;
John 8:36; 1 Corinthians 6:20; Colossians 2:15;
Hebrews 5:9; 1 John 2:2 & Revelation 5:12**

"Jesus Lives Forever"

As God's child, I am to make disciples, and them, to diligently teach
about the Lord's death and resurrection, and about those we are to reach.

Sometimes it may seem God is silent, but we are still to trust His Word;
He has ALWAYS been able to meet our EVERY need that has occurred.

I continue to watch His stunning power continually operating on earth,
AND I think about how He got here—when Mary provided His birth.

Because of God's great love, Jesus was born into the imperfect human race,
to die for humanity, so to God, He could reconcile Christians, by His grace.

His sacrifice freely provided the way for us to live a life fully abundant;
Receive Jesus, is all I now ask of you, so I will NOT sound redundant.

God's Holy Son lived in the flesh of a mortal body for thirty-three years;
He was sinless, died for our sins, rose again, and THEN, came our cheers!

Because He rightfully lives forever—as followers of Him, so will we;
In heaven, we will serve God AND live with Him—for ALL eternity!

**Luke 2:7, 11; John 1:1, 14; John 10:10; Romans 10:9-10;
2 Corinthians 5:1; 1 Thessalonians 4:17; Revelation 7:15;
Revelation 21:3 & Revelation 22:3**

"Jesus' Shed Blood"

Thank You, Father God, for the blood of Jesus,
how He lived, died, AND rose again to redeem us.

I ask You, in faith, to open the eyes of my heart to see
the many gifts the sinless blood of Jesus has provided me.

I have been washed in the Lord's powerful work anew,
because I heard about His resurrection, and I believe it's true!

Thank you, Lord Jesus, for Your blood You freely gave for me;
I sing praises to You, for Your perfect blood You shed on Calvary.

It is surely IN my heart, where my God-given faith has taken place;
Therefore, one day in the future, Lord, I will see Your precious face.

After every written prophecy is fulfilled, You will come for us SOON;
Then You can return any evening, or morning, or in ANY afternoon!

You are God's Living Word, who was born into THIS physical life;
You have taught me to be victorious, as well as to overcome strife.

Thank You for loving me and setting my formerly broken heart free;
Lord, You are now crowned in victory, and this, the world WILL see!

I humbly bow to You, my righteous Savior and my eternal Lord;
Thank You, in advance, for bringing me Your promised reward!

**Luke 23:33; John 3:16; John 8:32; Romans 10:9;
2 Corinthians 2:14; 2 Corinthians 5:15;
Galatians 3:13 & Revelation 22:4, 12**

"Let Our Lights Shine"

The children of the Most High God are to let our lights shine so bright,
so that everything in us sparkles, even when the sun goes down at night.

We now have victory in Jesus, and we radiate with a beautiful glow;
Illuminate His presence before others—so, He too, they may know.

Those who are against any of God's chosen people will be put to shame;
They don't stand a chance, because they don't know our Savior's name.

In my heart, I solemnly choose to maintain peace, and rest,
so that I may allow God's life-giving power, in me, to manifest.

Lord, You are my Light AND my Salvation, so I have no one to fear;
Nothing against THIS child of God should dare to EVER come near.

The enemy's deadly destructions came to a sure and permanent end,
when the redeeming blood of Jesus, my God, so lovingly DID send.

God, thanks for filling our mouths with laughter and lips with rejoicing,
so ALL Christians can always praise our One and ONLY righteous King!

**Job 8:21; Psalms 9:3, 6; Psalms 27:1; Psalms 32:11;
Psalms 34:5; Psalms 104:15; Isaiah 41:11;
Hosea 9:7; Matthew 5:16; John 15:16; Acts 4:10-12;
1 Corinthians 15:57 & Colossians 2:15**

"Merry Christmas"

Some people do call this a holiday, but it is REALLY Christmas;
Jesus was born on earth to set us free—this is why He came to us.

God sent His Son Jesus, which showed us His amazing glory;
My friends—Jesus' coming is the TRUE Christmas story!

Jesus, who is God, was born and placed very lovingly in a manger;
He came to earth to save all who believe in Him, from eternal danger.

Instead of intensely focusing on tangible presents of red and green,
Christians can look for Jesus' return because He will soon be seen.

He will annihilate the burdens of the rugged road for you and me;
From all pain and bondage, the Lord will supernaturally set us free!

"Merry Christmas" to everyone who has already escaped from sin,
by being transferred into God's kingdom when you were born again!

**Luke 2:10-14; John 1:1, 14; John 3:16; John 8:36;
John 10:10; Acts 1:11; Ephesians 1:7; Colossians 1:13
& Revelation 22:12**

"My Future"

My eternal future will be exceedingly great and overwhelmingly bright;
Forever, I'll be in God's magnificent kingdom, where Jesus is its light.

I will be so honored to thank God for every good thing He has done,
through His extravagant love He offered me, by the death of His Son.

As a result of the triumphant victory of my Lord and Savior Jesus,
as a Christian, my future is secure because of all He has done for us.

Every good thing God said over me has occurred; the bad is in the past,
and the eternal victory He has promised me will be fulfilled—at last!

**Job 22:28; Psalms 79:13; Isaiah 55:11; Matthew 9:29;
John 3:16; 2 Corinthians 1:20; 1 Thessalonians 2:13;
Colossians 2:15; 1 Peter 2:24 & Revelation 21:4, 23**

"My Prayer"

I genuinely need Your manifested presence, My Abba Father, right away;
I ask for Your grace to continually work in me, in Jesus' name, I pray.

Help me to know how to pray fervently, and let my requests be meek;
I want my prayer to be sincere, and to attract those You earnestly seek.

Lord, You intricately know everything that is within my heart each day;
You are already aware of what is there, before any word I imply, or say.

Yet, I pray for the wisdom I need, so in others, I can make a difference;
I desire to show them that a life, without You, defies common sense.

I want to reveal Your truth to each person who needs to learn quite a bit;
I pray YOUR light will shine brightly, to draw others to You, who see it!

**Psalms 44:21; Psalms 139:4; Isaiah 66:18;
Matthew 5:16; Matthew 7:8 & James 1:5**

"My Savior's Treasure"

Thank You, Father, for the delicious food I am receiving tonight;
I also want to praise You for making ALL things work out alright.

Almighty God, I genuinely love You with my whole heart today;
My affection for You is intensifying more than I can even say.

I thank You for working ALL situations out for my good,
and for causing them to benefit me, as You said they would.

Thanks for my complete healing, and for removing all poverty;
Thank You for taking every evil curse FAR AWAY from me.

It brings me inexpressible JOY that I am unable to measure,
to know I am not damaged goods—BUT, my Savior's treasure!

Exodus 19:5; Romans 8:28; Romans 11:17;
Galatians 3:13; Philippians 4:19 & James 1:17

"Nothing Holds Us Back"

Nothing can hold us back forever when God is for us, or on our side;
He has already declared our victory, so get ready for an awesome ride.

Our Savior lifts us gracefully like an eagle soars up into the sky;
He lifts us above the problems—because He loves us, is why.

He ALWAYS leads us in triumph, not just every once in a while;
With our success guaranteed, we CAN confidently choose to smile.

The Lord Jesus came to give us life, FULL and abounding,
so I say, "God's love for His people is absolutely astounding!"

Our triumph is the promise of which the Lord HAS already spoken;
Believe Him, and His Words of your success will not ever be broken!

**Psalms 18:48; Psalms 89:34; Isaiah 40:31; Mark 5:36;
John 3:16; 2 Corinthians 2:14 & 1 Thessalonians 2:13**

"Obedience Produces Blessings"

After Abram's name became Abraham, he walked in God's blessing;
Of the deep spiritual truths in this matter, I cannot be second-guessing.

Each time God gives any of His children a command with a promise,
our obedience to Him won't let us, His pre-ordained blessing, to miss.

God gives us opportunities, because EVERY person, He does love;
He is surely a gentleman; therefore, NO human, will He ever shove.

We can willingly submit to Him, and eternal salvation we will partake;
However, if we do not obey Him, we will create a never-ending mistake!

Our obedience to God will let Him give us plenty of good food to eat,
but the disobedient person—unquenchable flames of fire—will meet.

God's plans for believers will come to pass AS IF they are set in stone;
We can LET Him have His way—or we can just merely cry, or groan!

**Deuteronomy 11:27; 1 Kings 2:3; Proverbs 13:13;
Isaiah 1:19; Isaiah 55:11; Matthew 3:12; Matthew 7:24-27;
Luke 11:28; Luke 16:23; Romans 8:29-30; Galatians 3:6-9;
Hebrews 5:9 & James 1:25**

"Over a Rainbow"

Eternity in heaven will not be spent over a rainbow or in any strange way;
Christians will be with Jesus forever, which will be MORE than okay.

New Jerusalem will come, adorned as a bride all dressed for the part;
Then we will be made as one, with God, because of our changed heart.

We will receive the water of life, without ANY monetary payment,
because we accepted Jesus as our Lord; He's the One the Father sent.

Although the time we will spend with our Lord Jesus won't be a lullaby,
Christians asleep in Christ AND those on earth will meet Him in the sky!

Isaiah 55:1; Matthew 28:20; John 14:3;
John 17:21; 1 Thessalonians 4:17
& Revelation 21:2-6

"Perfect Peace Is in God"

When I keep my mind focused on God, He keeps me in perfect peace;
As I meditate daily in His Word, His favor and blessing He will release.

I ask my Father when I speak with powerful words in the Spirit today,
for the interpretation of what I said to be received, in Jesus' name, I pray.

God completely fulfills the desires of those who reverently fear Him;
He hears their cry for Jesus and miraculously chooses to save them.

The Father delights in us, and when we respect Him, He takes pleasure,
so much that He even searches every heart, to find one He can treasure.

Our Savior delights in beautifying the humble with everlasting salvation;
Bow yourself in respect to Him, and get yours, with GREAT expectation.

He is a mighty and glorious Lord, whom we WILL ALWAYS serve;
He showers us with love, health, and wealth—more than we deserve!

**Psalms 145:19; Psalms 149:4; Isaiah 26:3;
Jeremiah 17:10; Romans 3:24; Romans 5:6-8;
1 Corinthians 14:13 & Revelation 22:3**

"Power in God's Word"

Do you see yourself with the answers you seek?
Is your inner-vision lining up with God's Word?
Re-adjust YOUR thinking, to ONLY believe
the truths from Jesus' lessons you have heard.

The strength is in each of the Lord's teachings,
but we MUST believe every Word He said is true.
His awesome power is now working in my life;
If you believe, His truth will also work for YOU.

To the degree we truly believe in our Savior,
everything we genuinely need will be done.
Denying worldly things, AND trusting God
for everything, is becoming MUCH more fun!

**Matthew 8:13; Mark 5:36;
Mark 11:23 & Titus 1:2**

"Praising God in Heaven"

I am at peace, for my Lord protects me with favor, as a shield;
On the inside of me, is where He has been so clearly revealed.

It truly brings me considerable comfort to genuinely know
that my loving Savior is always with me, everywhere I go.

I walk with Him right now, although God, I cannot yet see;
Nonetheless, I am now at peace because Jesus lives IN me.

I know within me He resides because I opened the door up;
Now the two of us can ALWAYS eat together (dine or sup).

Forever with the Lord, thankfully, I will ALWAYS be;
I'll be praising my God, in heaven, for ALL eternity!

If you want to go, too, believe in Jesus and let Him come in;
He WILL accept you, AND He will free you from your sin!

**Exodus 33:20; Psalms 5:12; Psalms 79:13;
Psalms 145:2; Matthew 7:8; John 6:37, 51;
Romans 10:9-10; Ephesians 1:6-7;
Hebrews 13:5 & Revelation 3:20**

"Receiving Freedom"

It's time for all Christians to begin Receiving Freedom NOW;
Sin is what we ARE FREE from—through Jesus' blood, is how.

I am going to our big reunion with the FULL manifestations;
Each family member is waiting patiently, with eager expectations.

My faithful and benevolent God will NOT let me down, either,
for my Lord, Jesus has already proven Himself as my Healer!

The harvest is also prepared for you; it's ready today!
Receive whatever you need, NOW—don't delay!

The splendid glory of Almighty God is why I am still here;
I'm Receiving Freedom now, by putting my faith into gear!

My Lord once told me my faith had made me well;
Now that I receive it, I have a BETTER story to tell!

**Job 22:28; Psalms 146:7; Matthew 9:22, 29;
Romans 6:18; 1 Peter 2:24; Colossians 3:23
& 2 Timothy 2:2**

"Say 'No' to Suicide and 'Yes' to Jesus"

Are you silently screaming for help deep down, on the inside?
Do you find yourself, from others, wanting to run away or hide?

If you're on the verge of giving up and think you want to die,
don't fall for the enemy's scheme, by believing his malicious lie.

don't allow the demons to win your eternal soul, by giving in to them;
Give yourself wholly to the Lord, by placing your faith and trust in Him.

The borders of hell, created for demons, have been made very broad,
to also capture the people who reject the Lord JESUS, who is God.

Living in hell with Satan and his hateful demons for all eternity,
was not God's original plan or how He designed "forever" to be.

God's purpose for Christians is for us all to be like His glorious Son,
which WILL happen to us, after this place called earth, we are done.

However, the people who destroy their temple or their human body
will ALSO be destroyed by the Lord God, who is THE Almighty.

Therefore, just say "No" to suicide AND "Yes" to Jesus;
To give us life forever (with Him) is why He was sent to us.

Suicide is not your way to beat any disease, including cancer;
The way to truly live is through Jesus; He is THE ANSWER!

Just say "Yes" to Jesus and receive Him as your ONLY Lord,
then instead of hell, you will go to heaven AND get a reward!

**Isaiah 5:14; John 1:1, 12, 14; John 10:10; John 14:6;
1 Corinthians 3:17; Philippians 3:21
& Revelation 22:12**

"Seated in Christ"

My Christian family and I are seated in heavenly places in Christ Jesus;
God placed us there, so FROM eternity in hell, He could release us.

God's children ARE redeemed from every trap of the sneaky fowler,
by the precious blood of Jesus—from the hands of Satan, the prowler.

When Christians dwell with the Lord, no good thing at all will we lack,
for His protecting arms keep us safe with Him—away from any attack.

Abundant life for our family and friends is my official declaration today;
Lord, thanks for giving me the wisdom to know what else I should say.

WITH expectancy, I am opening my mouth wide so it, You may fill,
as I am becoming the person I am to be, while accomplishing Your will.

I know that the Lord our God, with salvation, will beautify the humble;
We can KNOW we are right, without having to prove it or to mumble.

Such knowledge requires wisdom from God to obtain this understanding;
We release God's power, and upon ourselves, we are NOT demanding!

**Psalms 34:10; Psalms 81:10; Psalms 91:3; Psalms 149:4;
Proverbs 2:6; Proverbs 3:5-6; Proverbs 4:7; Isaiah 63:12;
John 10:10; Ephesians 1:7; Ephesians 2:6; Philippians 2:14
& 1 Thessalonians 2:13**

"Seeds of Life"

The fruit is coming to its full maturity—this, I can now see;
It's springing forth from the words of life, arising out of me.

Salvation, wholeness, and restoration are sprouting all-day long
in the lives of others, because God's Words, from me, are strong.

Every seed will grow to maturity—each one will live and not die;
They have God-given eternal power, is the apparent reason why.

Because I speak His truth and also believe the words I say,
my activated faith allows my Lord and Savior to have His way.

God truly desires for every man, woman, and child to be free,
to inherit eternal life in Him, and to HAVE life abundantly!

**Job 22:28; Isaiah 55:11; Matthew 9:29;
Mark 11:23; Luke 8:11; John 10:10; 1 Peter 1:25;
2 Peter 3:9 & 1 John 2:14**

"Set Free"

In strength, You did guide Your people with such an amazing grace;
Forever You will let Your people be with You in Your glorious place.

When the horses and their riders were thrown into the Red Sea
is the victorious day, the people of God were physically set free.

However, their minds were stuck—they were quite stiff-necked, too;
They did not FULLY believe God's love for them was genuine, or true.

The Israelites ate manna in the wilderness every day for forty years;
Despite all of their ungrateful whining, God put up with their tears.

As long as Moses held his hands up high in the air, Israel prevailed,
but when he let them down—with joyful voices, their enemies yelled.

Aaron and Hur held up Moses' arms until the setting of the sun,
so in triumph, they defeated the enemy; the battle was all done!

Whatever the thing is that has been troubling or bothering you,
cast this care on God, and you will be amazed at what He will do!

**Exodus 15:13, 21; Exodus 16:35;
Exodus 17:11-13; Psalms 23:6 & 1 Peter 5:7**

"Speeches and Paintings"

Giving an eloquent speech can be like creating a magnificent painting;
They both will leave the audience amazed AND can be entertaining.

All the lovely painted strokes combined—make an impressive scene,
as the composition of well-spoken words produces a memorable theme.

The picture or the creative literature can embed into a person's mind,
capture their ingenuity, and keep them—artistically—from going blind.

These creative gifts come from the Almighty Father who is up above;
He gave us the power to create as He did and told us to walk in love.

Are you looking at the situations you are creating with each word?
To speak words that kill, while expecting life, would be absurd!

Job 22:28; Proverbs 18:21; Ephesians 5:2 & James 1:17

"Stand Still and Watch God"

The battle is NOT yours—it's God's, so JUST stand still,
even if the pressure begins to make you think it's all uphill.

Please REMEMBER, you do NOT have to fight;
for you, God will surely make things work out right.

Our Father WANTS His children to soar exceptionally high;
He wants us to help others succeed when they reach for the sky.

Don't worry about anything—trust God, AND don't fret;
Put thoughts of victory in your mind, and keep them set.

God loves You, and He will NOT ever fail,
so set your flags up high—it's TIME to sail!

Your heavenly Father has now opened the blessing doors;
Just confidently walk through, for the victory is yours!

**Deuteronomy 11:19; 2 Chronicles 20:15, 17;
Psalms 18:30; Ecclesiastes 4:9-10;
Luke 10:30-35; Romans 8:28; Romans 15:2;
2 Corinthians 2:14; Galatians 6:10;
Ephesians 1:3; Philippians 4:6-7
& 1 Timothy 6:17**

"Stand Still and Watch God, Thirteen Years Later"

My God-given miraculous life is not uphill any longer;
I am a new creation in Christ, who is growing stronger.

My optimism about the Lord's deliverance is increasing each day,
because of the words in my dream, I once heard Him audibly say.

My hand opened twice, as He told me my faith had made me well;
On the thirteenth anniversary of this dream, I was set free from hell.

This happened on my youngest brother's birthday of double four;
I'm sure God has given me victory, and I WON'T be poor anymore.

These doubles mean, to me, God's power will SOON be revealed;
I declare people will see, by the stripes of Jesus—I AM HEALED!

It's time to be still and to watch God do mighty miracles through me,
as He did through Moses, when He supernaturally parted the Red Sea!

**Genesis 41:32; Exodus 14:21; Job 22:28;
Matthew 9:29 & 1 Peter 2:24**

"Stay Attached to Christ"

Call upon Him, and He will answer by telling you what you don't know;
If you obey God's spoken Words, they will keep you from the pit below.

The Bible tells us, as MUCH as possible, to be in peace with all men;
When we love our God, we respect Him, so we won't intentionally sin.

Our dispute is NOT with the person who slanders or causes us strife;
We must open our eyes and SEE it's the devil who is attacking our life.

The enemy tried to scare me by saying I would undoubtedly go to hell,
but this was told to hinder me from sharing Jesus, about whom I do tell.

Whoever causes you trouble will fall down and not be able to rise again;
He will be overcome by calamity AND fall into a trap, like a lion's den.

It's unwise for one to fight against God's anointed and precious child;
It opens the door in the angry person's life, for the enemy to go wild.

As long as you choose to stay attached to Christ, who is your source,
you will remain steadfast in God's triumphant victory—of course!

By the power of the blood of Jesus, God always causes us to succeed,
so remember, child of God, He WILL definitely meet YOUR every need!

**Proverbs 24:16; Jeremiah 33:3; Luke 11:28; John 14:15;
Romans 12:18; 2 Corinthians 2:14; 2 Corinthians 10:3;
Ephesians 1:3 & Philippians 4:19**

"Thank You, Lord"

Thank You, Lord, for our eyes, ears, arms, legs, and two feet,
our mouths, and for our hands to shake with others we meet.

Thank You that we can taste the delicious food You always provide;
Thank You for our great transportation, which gives us an enjoyable ride.

Thank You for Your love AND Your abundant comfort and provision,
for clean air, heat, water, the dishwasher, and EVEN for our television.

Thank You for our family, friends, neighbors, and the comfort You give;
Thank You for the cross where You died so that every Christian can live.

Thank you, Jesus, for revealing to each Christian that You are God's Son;
Thank You for Your obedience on the cross, and ALL You have done!

**Psalms 139:13; Philippians 2:8; Philippians 4:19;
Ephesians 3:20; Colossians 2:14; 1 Thessalonians 5:18
& 1 John 2:2**

"The Cross"

Thank you, Father, for the atoning blood of Jesus that was shed for me;
Thank you for saving, healing, AND supernaturally setting me FREE.

I am grateful for the sacrifice of YOUR sinless Son on Calvary;
All praise belongs to my Lord for bringing me complete victory.

Thank You, Jesus, for allowing the nails to go into Your hands and feet,
for the way You rose three days later to make a way, for us, so sweet.

Now other people have the opportunity to see the change that came,
which first happened after I prayed, in faith, in Your victorious name.

I am genuinely delighted I am not going to get the death in hell, I deserve;
This is only ONE of the great truths in the gospel I have come to observe.

God has placed His mark on me—since I am a Christian, I am sealed;
Now I am helping Christ, in other repentant believers, to be revealed!

**Mark 15:25; John 14:15, 21; Acts 4:12; Romans 3:23;
Romans 6:23; Romans 10:9; 2 Corinthians 1:22;
2 Corinthians 5:17-21 & Ephesians 1:7, 13**

"Traffic Lights"

In this country, the traffic light's color tells us if we must stop or go;
The same in God's kingdom, to the left or right, the Lord, will us, show.

Dear reader, I pray for it to be the right way you will deliberately choose;
My prayer is for you to follow the Lord Jesus, so you may NEVER lose.

Furthermore, let Him direct you, and He definitely will help you to excel;
However, to turn AWAY from the Lord would inevitably lead you to hell.

Thoroughly kick out all sin from among you, which is as the leaven,
and then, IF you obey the Lord, you will live WITH Him, in heaven.

Developing a relationship with Him NOW will allow you to be free at last;
Time in heaven with God FOREVER seems as if it WILL be a BLAST!

When you see the Lord Jesus, He will give unto you your earned reward,
and then, daily in His temple, you will ALWAYS be serving the Lord!

**Isaiah 30:21; Matthew 4:19; Matthew 7:25; Luke 11:28;
John 8:36; John 14:21, 23, 25; Revelation 7:15;
Revelation 20:10; Revelation 21:3-4 & Revelation 22:12**

"We Always Win!"

My Lord is a shield for me, my glory, and He lifts up my head;
He delivers me from every affliction, and He eliminates all dread.

I didn't die, but I still live and gladly declare the works of my Lord;
I am thankful now for all He's done—and in the future, for my reward.

Jesus' perfectly demonstrated steps are truthfully my only real pathway,
which will lead me to God—where forevermore, WITH Him, I will stay.

Many are called by our loving God, but only the chosen ones does He pick;
We must lead others to Jesus now because He will come speedily or quick!

God gives supernatural power to Christians, and He makes each of us strong;
This strength He gives us lets us fight our enemies AND win, ALL day long!

As long as we remain in the Lord—because He is continually for us,
in Him, every battle WILL end in triumph—for we ARE victorious!

**Psalms 3:3; Psalms 16:11; Psalms 68:35; Psalms 85:13;
Psalms 86:15; Psalms 118:17; Matthew 16:27; Matthew 20:16;
Romans 5:8; 2 Corinthians 2:14; Philippians 4:13, 19 &
Colossians 2:15**

"Welcome Home"

God certainly does not intend for you to live by yourself or all alone;
He will guide you and satisfy your needs, for, on you, His favor is shown.

God genuinely loves you and truly demands to be YOUR only Lord;
He wants to forgive every person AND give us all an eternal reward.

Believe that good things will happen to your friends and family, too,
but don't stop there; press into God's Word and LET it work for YOU!

Be immensely courageous, and God will surely strengthen your heart;
Grow close to Him, and He will give you an impressive NEW start.

When you give yourself freely to God, success will come soon;
The sound it's beginning to make is a beautiful and vibrant tune.

With your attentive ears, listen to what the Spirit is saying;
"Go back to Jesus, now," is what I hear Him loudly playing.

I gladly welcome you to Almighty God's righteous throne;
It is great you chose to humble yourself, and have come home.

To those who have returned, you will sing of the Lord's mercies forever;
I think the brilliant way He brought you back to Him is quite clever!

**Psalms 5:12; Psalms 31:24; Isaiah 58:11; Luke 4:8;
2 Corinthians 2:14; 2 Corinthians 5:17;
2 Peter 3:9 & 1 John 4:8**

"Who Is Christ Jesus, the Son?"

Jesus is the Word, who was with the Father in the beginning,
who dwelt among us AND is our soon-coming righteous King.

He is the powerful, omnipotent, omnipresent Ruler, who beat His enemy,
and WILL valiantly rule all kingdoms—so the inferior kings WILL flee.

He is the Lord who is FULLY God, yet He was fully man, as well;
The One whose blood redeems AND rescues each Christian, from hell.

He was conceived of the Holy Spirit by Mary, who was a teenage virgin;
Her obedience to God permits Him to save His people from our every sin.

His righteousness for our unpardonable sin was completely exchanged;
Therefore, after our conversion—from God, we are no longer estranged.

Jesus is the anointed Son, sent by the Father to give life to us on this earth;
Life is offered to all who believe in His death and resurrection, after His birth.

He is the Lord who paid for my salvation, AND my body was healed;
My profession of Him allows me to get saved, and God's power revealed!

**Matthew 9:29; Mark 13:26; Luke 1:33; Luke 2:7, 10;
John 1:1, 14; John 3:16; Acts 17:7; Romans 10:9;
Ephesians 1:7, 13; Colossians 1:13; 1 Peter 2:24;
1 John 2:2; Revelation 11:15 & Revelation 22:20**

"Who Is God, the Father?"

He is the Father, the Holy Spirit, as well as the Son;
Each Christian's God is all three of these persons in one.

He is our only true source for every provision we ever receive;
His requirement for our blessing is: in His Son Jesus, we believe.

He is the ruler of all things, and in Him is where we truly live,
He made eternal life possible for us when His Son, He did give.

Have you received Jesus as your Lord? Do you know Him today?
No person the Father gives to Jesus will be cast out or turned away!

**Psalms 18:2; Psalms 47:6; Psalms 96:1; Psalms 139:1-24;
John 1:12; John 3:16; John 6:37; John 10:30; Acts 17:7, 28;
Romans 5:1; 1 Corinthians 2:10-11; 1 Corinthians 8:6;
1 Corinthians 12:7-11; Ephesians 1:7; Philippians 4:19;
Colossians 1:16; Colossians 2:15;
1 Peter 2:24 & 1 John 5:7**

"Who Is the Holy Spirit?"

Who is the Holy Spirit? He's part of God—He is in the Trinity;
When Jesus ascended to the Father, God's Spirit was sent to me.

He lives in me now, and He shows me what is to come so that I won't fear;
He teaches me everything I need to know; therefore, He is welcome here.

In this life on earth, the Holy Spirit gives us our comfort, so satisfying,
because we are connected to Jesus; He is each Christian's righteous King.

The Holy Spirit is who raised the Lord Jesus from His atoning death,
and He gives ALL obedient Christians wisdom in life, in our every breath.

We are sealed in Him until our redemption day, which is so glorious,
because the Father, Son, AND Holy Spirit HAVE made us victorious!

**Isaiah 26:3; Mark 10:45; John 1:1, 14; John 16:7, 13;
Acts 17:7; Romans 8:11; 2 Corinthians 2:14;
1 John 2:2, 27; 1 John 4:10 & 1 John 5:7**

"Wipe the Tears from Our Eyes"

One day soon, the devil will be bound,
but my freedom in Jesus is already found.

I will gladly praise the Lord Almighty today,
for paying the enormous bill, I could NOT pay.

My eternal salvation is not paid by what I can do;
Jesus' sinless blood purchased it for me—and you.

The Savior, Jesus, obediently bore the stripes for our every sin;
He willingly went to hell for us—so we could be born again.

Three days after His death, Christ Jesus did victoriously rise;
Therefore, in the future, God will wipe the tears from our eyes!

**Mark 16:6; John 3:16; Acts 2:31-32; 1 Corinthians 6:20;
1 Peter 2:24; 1 John 2:2; Revelation 20:2
& Revelation 21:4**

"Wise as a Serpent"

Be wise as a serpent, but harmless as a dove;
Be kind to the needy—and daily walk in love.

There's turmoil on the earth, so Christians need wisdom today
about the things now, AND later, we are free from—right away.

Jesus came to earth to give believers in Him life abundantly;
Therefore, with thanks, I choose to live in this place joyfully.

I share my precious Lord's love with many others:
neighbors, friends, strangers, and even my brothers.

However, to know who I can trust, I MUST be wise,
because some people may be bad BUT are in disguise!

**Psalms 16:11; Matthew 10:16; John 3:16; John 10:10;
1 Corinthians 11:1; 2 Corinthians 11:13; Ephesians 4:32;
Ephesians 5:2; 1 Thessalonians 5:18; James 5:19-20
& Revelation 20:10**

"You Will Receive What You Need"

My Savior's blood He willingly shed was purchased for me;
His generous sacrifice was given so He could forever set me free.

In my heart is where real God-given faith does commence to take place;
I am convinced that one day I will get to see my Lord Jesus, face to face.

Nonetheless, while I am here on earth, there is work for me to do,
so many things I have to accomplish BEFORE I will be through.

Jesus said each time I lay my hands on the people who are sick,
the ones who believe, will recover—and often it is certainly quick.

When I speak to the monstrous mountain, and I demand it to move,
it has no other choice, but of my authoritative command to PROVE.

I know my God's infallible Word for all humanity is eternally true;
I depend on Him, and I believe His Word will ALSO work for you.

If in your heart, you choose to completely accept His Word and believe,
soon you will find—whatever it is you NEED, you, too, WILL receive!

**Psalms 61:7; Mark 11:23-24; Mark 16:18; John 3:16;
Acts 20:28; 1 Corinthians 6:20; Philippians 4:19;
1 Thessalonians 2:13 & Revelation 22:4**

Personal Poems

✝

"A Man Named Thomas"

While I was at the grocery store nearby, I met a doubting, Thomas;
I told him about my heavenly Father, and I shared His eternal promise.

I told this kind and humble man about how much God really loved him;
I gave my spiffy friend a brand-new compact Bible—it was very slim.

I told him we don't become God's child based on OUR merit or good;
We are saved, by God's grace, by putting faith in Jesus, as we all should.

After he understood the message of the cross, to God, he gratefully said,
"In my heart, I believe You raised Your Son JESUS up from the dead.

I confess Jesus as my Lord, and my way to You He triumphantly paved;
Because of Jesus' sinless blood, I am declared righteous, and I am saved!"

You who call Jesus "Lord", and believe God raised Him from the grave,
will escape from destruction in hell, because you, too, He WILL save!

John 3:16; Romans 10:9-10 & Ephesians 2:8

"Bob and His Job"

Father, today I pray You will help Bob, at his job not at all to be stressed;
I ask You to help him focus on the truth that, in Christ Jesus, he is blessed.

This man has a nice, beautiful wife and an extremely loving family, too,
but please show him how to keep his attention focused ONLY on You.

The position You have blessed him with allows him his family to feed;
His income also provides EVERYTHING his young children need.

My heart cries, "When Bob is working, help him keep his mind set free,
knowing the work he does is for YOU, and NOT just for his company."

I bless him with Your peace that continually passes our understanding,
which will help him daily, especially when his job becomes demanding.

Bob has a safe place to work, and something he can put his hands to,
but when it's time for another career, please show him what he must do.

In the name of my magnificent Lord Jesus, I now choose to pray,
believing these prayers of mine will be heard AND answered today!

**Matthew 7:7-8; Mark 11:24; Ephesians 1:3;
Philippians 4:7 & Colossians 3:23**

"Candice"

Shortly after I obeyed my Lord's leading to call myself "Candice"
it was as if me, my Lord and Savior began to passionately kiss.

Although I do live by THE faith of my righteous Lord Jesus, today,
God's blessings are better than any thoughts I may struggle to convey.

He is an amazing God, who is greater than I can express;
He saved me from hell, although I was a tangled mess.

During this life that I live on earth now, throughout ALL eternity,
forever, I will thank and praise Him for what He's done for me.

My sincere heartfelt question today is, "What about you?
Will you be invited to live with the Lord Jesus, too?"

Please call on Him right now, while you still can,
because God wants to save EVERY woman and man.

By faith, call on Jesus as your Lord—He's the Father's Son;
Believe He is alive AND of His covenant-changing resurrection.

Then you can genuinely repent to God for your every sin,
and undoubtedly, heaven—one day, YOU will enter in!

You will be VERY blessed by God, as well,
for you will most assuredly be saved from hell!

**Psalms 79:13; Luke 15:20; John 3:16;
Acts 3:19; Romans 10:9-10;
1 Corinthians 1:30; Galatians 2:20;
2 Peter 3:9 & Revelation 22:12**

"Daddy, oh Daddy"

Daddy, oh daddy, how I earnestly pray you will believe the things I said when I told you about Jesus' resurrection, and how He arose from the dead.

He is the Son of God, seated at the right hand of the Majesty on High, and one day VERY soon, He will meet His joyous saints in the sky.

His people will live with Him forever; we will walk on His street of gold; God WILL renew our youth like an eagle, so we won't ever grow old.

The temperature will be perfect in heaven; if not, it would make us sad, and God's Word says there won't be any sorrow—so we should be glad.

Heaven is full of abounding love, and impressive beauty is all around; Here, Christians will forever sing God's praises, with a beautiful sound.

God wants you to be with Him, but first, He must change your heart; By removing your sin is how He is able to give you a brand-new start.

Your confession of Jesus as your Lord allows Him to wash away your sin; It justifies you in God's sight and will let Him invite YOU into heaven.

My desire is for you to receive Him now, BEFORE your final breath; I pray you will accept Him in your heart and escape from eternal death.

God has given you one LAST opportunity to accept His FINAL call, to make Jesus your Lord so that He can save you from a permanent fall.

Life or death is your decision; YOU decide which one you'll CHOOSE; I hope your destination will be with Jesus, and you—the devil will lose!

Deuteronomy 30:19; Psalms 103:5; Psalms 147:1; Matthew 7:21; Mark 16:6; John 3:16; Romans 10:9; 2 Corinthians 5:17; 1 Thessalonians 1:10; 1 Thessalonians 4:17; Hebrews 8:1; Revelation 1:5 & Revelation 21:3-4, 21

"For God's Glory"

A bowed up arm, a crippled leg, a blinded eye that could not see,
but my faithful God had His mighty hand so lovingly upon me.

The doctor said three times I would not live; he did not know why,
but before this tragic event occurred, God told me I would not die.

Later—in my dream, I saw my immobile hand open AND close;
The Almighty saw me among the people, then me, He rightly chose.

He told me my faith HAS MADE me well—or let me be healed;
I am to allow God's power, through Jesus, always to be revealed.

I have discovered, every Christian's victory is in our Lord Jesus;
We need to remember, by grace, He paid the price to redeem us.

I am here to give hope to others in their desperate time of need,
by sharing my righteous Lord Jesus—the Father's faithful seed!

God revealed to me the reason I am alive and well, is for His glory,
and that, dear friend, is just the FIRST part of my amazing story!

**Psalms 139:5; Mark 11:24; John 1:1, 14; John 11:4;
John 15:16; Ephesians 1:7; Ephesians 2:8;
Philippians 2:13 & 1 Peter 2:24**

"God Has Good Messages"

After I lost too much blood, I had to have a blood transfusion;
It occurred from a chiropractic adjustment, which caused confusion.

Although the devil tried his best to annihilate me—to kill me that day,
I'm still alive because God has many messages He wants me to convey.

My first lesson, from God—my heartfelt, impressive thought,
is to let you know, by Jesus' perfect blood, YOU were bought.

His sinless blood and His obedience to God paid the price for our sin;
However, His blood ONLY saves those who choose to be born again!

To become another creation, to be refreshed AND re-created brand-new,
receive Jesus as your Lord, and believe He's alive, is what you must do.

This voluntary profession of faith from you who make it today,
WILL profoundly transform YOUR life, in a significant way.

You have become an entirely new creation, not made by any man,
but one who was created by Christ, as soon as your faith began.

Now, through your faith, by God's grace, you have been born again;
Since the Lord chose you, He will fight your battles, and you will win!

**Deuteronomy 20:4; John 10:10; John 15:16;
Romans 10:9-10; 1 Corinthians 6:20; 1 Corinthians 15:57;
2 Corinthians 2:14; 2 Corinthians 5:17; Ephesians 2:8;
Colossians 1:16; 2 Timothy 2:2; 1 Peter 5:8 & 1 John 2:2**

"Mama, oh Mama"

Mama, Oh Mama, I won't ever understand
why I'll never again see you upon this land.

I realize now that you are no longer here,
how much to my heart you were so dear.

All you ever wanted was your family's comfort and love;
I'm sorry you never quite got it, but you will from above.

I want to ask my great God, "Oh, why-oh, why"
but I have no right—He predestined you to die.

It's time to laugh, rejoice, and live with the Son,
for your work on the EARTH is over—it's done.

To those who are left, who mourn and who cry,
remember, to live with Christ—first, you must die.

It's time to laugh, rejoice, and live with the Son,
for your work on the EARTH is over—it's done!

**Psalms 16:11; Psalms 139:16; Ezekiel 37:26;
Colossians 3:3 & Galatians 2:20**

"My Faith Has Made Me Well"

God, You once told me my faith had made me well,
so I trust You will give me an outstanding story to tell.

I am fully aware that You did this AT LEAST once before
when You divinely healed a man I met, named Alan Moore.

I ask You, Lord, to help my unbelief in You right now;
I pray for my heart to follow wholly after You, somehow.

You, my righteous and faithful King, won't ever let me down,
so, in faith, my face wears a smile—NOT a menacing frown!

**Psalms 145:17; Matthew 7:7-8; Matthew 9:22;
Mark 9:24; Acts 17:7; 2 Corinthians 1:20;
1 Thessalonians 2:13 & Hebrews 13:5**

"My Friend John"

God, I have been thinking about my good friend, named John,
how much I genuinely loved him, and how long he's been gone.

He had a wife, two daughters, a son, and a few grandchildren, too;
I understand they loved him and still miss him, even more than I do.

I know he is with You now, ALL restored and sparkling new;
I'm sure he is happy because he's eternally abiding with YOU!

Thank You for our many in-depth and interesting Bible lessons,
and how he often asked me many thought-provoking questions.

I am grateful I will see my true friend one day again on high,
perhaps when I meet my Lord and Savior Jesus, in the sky!

**Psalms 16:11; 2 Corinthians 5:8;
Philippians 3:21 & 1 Thessalonians 4:17**

"My Miracle Story"

Let me tell you the true story about when my blood vessel broke;
I had a brain aneurysm, five brain surgeries, a seizure, and a stroke.

All of these events happened when I was only thirty-four years old;
I was too young to experience such tragedies, is what I have been told.

After a chiropractic adjustment, my head was aching, and it got intense;
Because I went straight home, my husband said, "You make NO sense."

"You need to go to the hospital," he repeatedly said;
"If you don't go now, then you just might end up dead."

"Let me have her, God. Please, let me have her," Satan cried;
"She belongs to me, and I have things for her to do," God replied.

An angel told me, "Don't worry; everything is going to be okay;
Jesus has triumphantly kicked His enemy (the devil) out of your way."

I endured many ordeals in the hospital for eighty long and arduous days;
However, this was when I began to learn about my God's GOOD ways.

I am abiding fully alive and well, in spite of the nurses and the doc;
I can confidently say, "I am STILL here because Jesus is my Rock!"

My point is this, whatever YOU are currently going through,
ask God (in faith) for your specific need, and He will also help you.

Today, I am no longer a wife; however, I am still a BLESSED mom;
If you want to know more, go to my website at **receivingfreedom.com**!

**Psalms 62:6; Colossians 2:15;
1 Peter 5:7 & 1 John 4:8**

"Now or Later"

I asked God for wisdom to know which poems to put in this book,
and which ones to publish next for people to read or take a look.

I also asked Him to show me the ones to release after I'm gone, later;
In each edition, He deserves credit for making the rhymes to be greater.

I thank the Father for His divine wisdom to put the pressure on me
that is now revealing the special anointing of His royal majesty!

The Joy of my Lord Jesus gives me the strength to overcome;
Because of Him, I am thankful for the person I have now become!

**Nehemiah 8:10; Psalms 143:5; Romans 4:25;
Ephesians 1:3; 1 Peter 2:24 & James 1:5**

"Prayer for My Children"

God, I pray for Your special blessings on my amazing children today;
I ask that any wrong thing I have ever done won't keep them away.

I invite You to spiritually draw them unto Your righteous right side,
so safely, now AND for all eternity, with You, they will joyfully abide.

Please let them know You are skillfully guiding them EVERY day,
and You are directing their steps, to the left or right, along the way.

Father, in Jesus' mighty name, I ask for Your answers, without delay;
I can request this because, for ALL of my sins, my Lord Jesus, did pay!

I am grateful for Your promise, they from You will never depart;
I praise You NOW for answering the prayers of this mother's heart!

**Proverbs 22:6; Isaiah 30:21; Matthew 7:7-8;
Matthew 28:20 & 1 John 2:2**

"Prayer for Our Leaders"

All Christians have been given divine orders sent down from above;
We MUST pray for our leaders AND genuinely show them our love.

Therefore, I pray for our President, his family, his staff, and all they do;
I pray for each leader in the world, and for the peace of Jerusalem, too.

Lord, forgive those in charge who have kicked You out of the schools;
I repent, on their behalf, for removing Your strict, yet necessary, rules.

I pray our country will go back to its godly AND humble beginning,
when people leaned on You and were not so proud of all their sinning.

Thank You, Father God, for hearing my prayer and answering me today;
I ask in Jesus' name, for our nation to return to You AND live Your way.

Yet, if I never see circumstances in this life become significantly greater,
I trust they will be better than I can imagine now, when I SEE you later!

**Psalms 122:6; Matthew 5:44; John 15:12;
1 Corinthians 2:9; 2 Corinthians 5:21; 1 Timothy 2:1-2;
1 John 5:14-15 & Revelation 22:4**

A Few
Fun Poems

✝

"My Refrigerator Makes Ice Cream"

Many happy children were running to the ice cream truck;
The supply quickly sold out, so the last boy was out of luck.

Then came a generous girl named Alison, to the rescue,
when she proudly proclaimed, "I WILL certainly help you!

My refrigerator makes ice cream, in chocolate or vanilla,
so you can pick your FAVORITE flavor, little fella."

"Thank you, my new friend, for being so kind,
I choose chocolate—I have made up my mind."

The cold and creamy flavors were tasty and pleasant,
especially to the lad, who was grateful for his present.

Every child was delighted about the delivery that came,
so they thanked God with a simple prayer, in Jesus' name!

James 1:17 & 1 Thessalonians 5:18

"The 8 x 10 Shed"

Today I was looking for a well-maintained 8 x 10 storage shed;
While I searched online—to Craigslist, I was surprisingly led.

God prompted a couple to decide, "With this building, we must depart,"
and they quickly knew this shed was meant for me—from the start.

As they listened to my miracle story with admiration, or unspeakable awe,
they were deeply moved by every hospital-glamor-shot picture they saw.

Then they each reverently and sincerely bowed their head;
I could sense in my heart, this spirited duo was being God-led.

I asked them how much we could purchase this nicely painted shed for;
The benevolent couple said, "Our heart's desire is NOT as before."

They enthusiastically searched AND quickly found the required key,
then said, "We're sowing a seed; we will move it for you, and it's free!"

**Proverbs 3:27; Proverbs 16:9; Luke 8:8;
Acts 20:35 & 2 Corinthians 9:12**

"Todd and Loose Vowels"

His stomach trouble made him repeatedly rush to the restroom;
The mess he made was cleaned with a mop, NOT with a broom.

He heard his mom compassionately say he had loose bowels,
but Todd thought she meant to say he had "loose vowels."

If the alphabet letters "A, E, I, O, and U" were loose,
he thought to himself, "Do I tie them up with a noose?"

Todd learned a lot about eating junk food that day;
He discovered it does MORE harm than tooth decay.

The next time he was offered something not good,
Todd said, "No, thanks; I'll eat an apple, as I should!"

God told us to be wise (to keep our body under control);
If asked, He gives us wisdom on what to put into our bowl.

We should also thank God for all of the food we eat,
whether it's a fruit, vegetable, carbohydrate, or meat!

**Proverbs 2:6; 1 Corinthians 9:27; Ephesians 5:15;
1 Thessalonians 5:18 & James 1:5**

Authoritative
Poems

✝

"Eviction Notice"

Enemy of God, also known as an infirmity or a cataract,
I command you to be removed and NEVER to come back!

Paralysis, in Jesus' MIGHTY name, I demand you to go, too;
Since I am speaking in faith, you know what you MUST do.

An eviction notice TODAY, to you, I do authoritatively give;
No more in my body will I allow you—or ANY illness to live.

By the power of the blood of Jesus, I am now perfectly healed;
His never-ending love for me has been dramatically revealed!

To You, Oh holy and righteous God, I choose to joyfully sing
of Your faithfulness AND Your love—my victorious King!

Thank You, my Lord, for supernaturally healing me,
And for allowing the whole world to hear AND see!

**Psalms 68:32; Psalms 136:1-2; Mark 11:23;
Acts 17:7; 1 Corinthians 15:57 & 1 Peter 2:24**

"The Healing Poem"

In the name of Jesus, I command sickness to flee;
You wicked Spirit of Infirmity, get off of that knee.

Remove yourself from that eye, tooth, neck, and back;
You are not allowed to cause another evil heart attack.

Devil, you have been hanging around TOO long, so GO today;
I speak this in Jesus' name; therefore, you MUST obey what I say!

From the tops of our heads to the bottom of our righteous feet,
we are blessed because, Satan—you, the Lord Jesus did beat!

We have been made whole by the sinless blood of the Lamb;
Enemy of God, you have been defeated by the GREAT "I Am!"

As God said in His Word of our success, I also victoriously decree,
"Child of the Most High, you are restored—you HAVE the victory!"

Body, Jesus paid all of your debts, for you to be completely healed;
Receive what you need and allow Christ in you to be fully revealed.

I speak health into your whole being, and I cast out all manner of strife;
Today, the mighty Word of God brings, to you, a refreshing NEW life!

I wash you in His blood—I declare you are now thoroughly set free;
I loose His Holy Spirit's anointing over you and ALL of your family!

**Job 22:28; Mark 11:23; Colossians 2:15;
James 4:7 & 1 Peter 2:24**

"Payment Demanded"

Satan, you are trespassing on God's property;
I bind you up and demand you to get off of me.

I confidently use my authority in Christ Jesus,
who died, so FROM you, He could release us.

I choose to take back everything you stole from me,
and I boldly declare I now have a seven-fold victory!

I demand your payment be made IN FULL today;
I expect to receive what belongs to me—right away!

**Proverbs 6:31; Matthew 10:1, 8;
Matthew 18:18; 1 Corinthians 3:23;
Ephesians 1:3; Philippians 4:19
& 2 Peter 1:3**

"The Promises in God's Word"

Don't consider the problem, but only the promises in God's Word;
Instead of believing the lie, choose to trust the truth you've heard.

The Lord has already promised to meet your EVERY need;
To get your provisions, read His written Word; it is the seed.

Just as the Almighty God, our Father Abraham chose to believe,
his lovely wife also perceived the truth, AND she did conceive.

Child of God, what things, good or bad, are you thinking about today?
Aligning your thoughts WITH God will kick the bad thoughts away.

Then when an evil spirit comes against you in an ugly way,
bind it up by speaking the words the Lord taught YOU to say.

Continue to stay in faith, as long as it takes—remain steadfast,
and you WILL see your victory sooner—or even later, at last!

Jesus said you would receive the faith-filled words you say,
so begin by speaking beneficial words (in faith)TODAY!

**Psalms 33:4; Matthew 18:18; Mark 11:23; Luke 8:11;
Luke 17:19; Romans 4:20; Philippians 4:8, 19;
Hebrews 11:11 & James 4:7**

"Victory Is Mine"

You lying cataract, I cast you into the billowing sea,
and I DEMAND you be removed FAR from me.

In the mighty name of Jesus, I use my authority today
and boldly command you to mind me—SO GO AWAY!

Since Jesus HAS defeated you—I declare, "This victory is mine,
and the evidence is being manifested—IT IS the appointed time."

I Will have whatever I say, is what my Lord Jesus promised me,
so I say, "Cataract, you are gone, and I can see PERFECTLY!"

Job 22:28; Mark 11:23 & 1 Peter 2:24

Salvation Information

✝

"Salvation"

Salvation demands that the Lord Jesus, to you, becomes very real;
Believe in AND acknowledge Him, so you, He can save AND heal.

Our deliverance can only be received by God's amazing grace;
By our OWN works is NOT how we can make it to His place.

Since God loved the world, He offered, for us, His only begotten Son;
Each person who believes in Jesus gets saved because of all HE has done.

The payment has been paid in full for every person's unrighteous sin;
What we must do is simply confess Jesus as our Lord, to enter heaven.

In our hearts, we must also believe God raised Jesus up from the grave;
Our belief and confession of Him as Lord allows our God, us, to save!

**Matthew 10:32; Luke 6:23; John 3:16; John 14:27;
Romans 10:9-10; 2 Corinthians 2:14; 2 Corinthians 5:21;
Ephesians 2:8 & 1 John 2:2**

"Prayer of Salvation"

If you do not know the Lord as your eternal Savior this day,
you will be God's child when you believe and repeat what I say:

"Dear Jesus, I believe You are God's ONLY begotten Son;
There is only one way to the Father—Lord, You are the One!

I believe You died for me, and three days later, You rose up again,
so I invite You into my heart and ask You to forgive ALL my sin.

Thank You for cleansing me, Jesus, for making me spotless and new;
I am a new creation, and accepted (by God) because I believe in YOU!"

**Matthew 3:2; John 1:12; John 14:6; Acts 16:31;
Romans 10:9; 2 Corinthians 5:17; Galatians 3:26;
Ephesians 1:6-7; 1 John 4:17 & Revelation 1:5**

Congratulations on your new life in Christ if you just received Jesus
as your Lord! To learn more, find a Christian church that teaches
that Jesus is the only way to the Father!

Jesus' atoning death would not have happened if there was another
way for our forgiveness (Matthew 26:39).

Also Available!

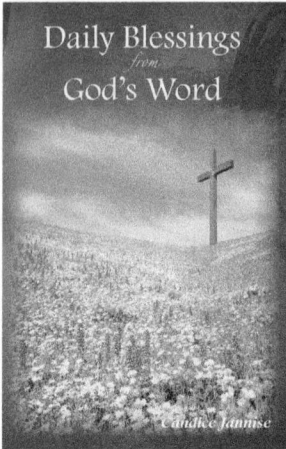

"Daily Blessings from God's Word" has three to five quoted scriptures for every day of the year that are quoted in a fun way! The Bible chapter number is matched to the month number. The Bible verse number is matched to the day. Each quote has an inspirational or teaching comment that follows. Some thoughts occasionally rhyme.

"Candice" is the autobiography of a Christian woman who grew up in China, Texas. As an adult, she survived a brain aneurysm, a blood transfusion, a seizure, five brain surgeries, and a paralyzing stroke. Although three times, the doctors said she would not live, Candice is still here today to tell you about God's genuine love for you. **"Candice"** will give you hope and help you trust God for whatever you need.

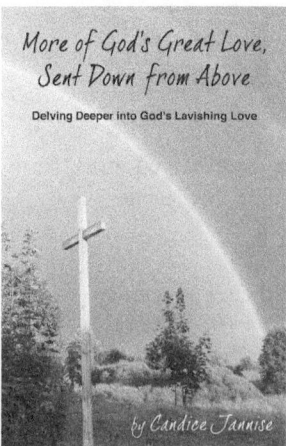

"More of God's Great Love, Sent Down from Above" is Candice's second Christian poetry book, which can help you go deeper into the truths of God in a meaningful way. The last chapter has vivid narrative poems about Bible characters, such as Moses, Joseph, and the apostle Paul.

About the Author

Born and raised in Texas, I am the tenth child, the eighth daughter of Cleveland and Ruth Jannise. I have seven sisters, three brothers, and many nieces and nephews, but most importantly, I have two grown children.

On October 28, 2004, a chiropractic adjustment caused me to have a brain aneurysm. When the doctors put a piece of metal (called a coil) in the blood vessel in my brain to stop it from leaking, my blood vessel ruptured and caused a stroke, which paralyzed the left side of my body. Details of my miraculous survival and recovery can be seen at:

www.receivingfreedom.com

Although the doctors said I would not live before each of the first three brain surgeries—after my cognitive ability returned, I wrote my first book, "Daily Blessings from God's Word".

Most of the poems I have written were given to me after I had five brain surgeries. More specifically, after I obeyed God to change churches, for reasons unknown to me. Within the first three months at the new church, I wrote more than one hundred Christian poems, for the glory of God.

These poems began after I heard the first rhyming lines in my head! Then, as my awesome Creator prompted me, I wrote whatever He said!

God also gave me a song I named "Jesus Broke the Chains", which is sung by my sister, Robin Sonnier, on her gospel CD, "Come As You Are". This uplifting CD is on my website's "Shop" page.

Child of God, remember, God loves you, despite what you have done, because, by His grace, He freed you from His wrath by the death of His Son!

"To the Readers"

To everyone who enjoys reading the words I wrote,
I send my blessings with this final teaching note.

If you genuinely desire to live life fresh and free,
obeying and trusting God will save you much misery.

The Lord God's pre-ordained plans for you are good;
Living His way will let them happen, as they should.

When things go wrong, remember, Satan is on the prowl,
watching, and waiting for you to sin—like a night owl.

Obey the Lord God by doing everything He said,
and you will never die—or WISH you were dead.

Your promised life with God, in the end, will always be,
without Satan or his demons, and FREE from misery!

**Proverbs 4:20-22; John 11:26;
1 Peter 5:8 & Revelation 21:4, 6**

Closing Comments

I pray the truths gleaned from the words in this poetry book will brighten **every** part of your life, including any portion of it that is currently filled with darkness.

My heartfelt prayer is that these poems will gently nudge you closer to the Lord. May they increase your desire to follow Him, and give you a revelation of who God is and the good plans He has already written for you (Psalms 139:16-17 and Jeremiah 29:11).

Get ready; Jesus is coming soon!

Candice

God Loves...You!

**The picture below is a thought-provoking display
of God's love for...you!**

**Do you understand the reason Jesus died was so God
could forgive the sins of everyone who believes
in Jesus and give eternal life to them?**